ORAL LANGUAGE AND COMPREHENSION IN PRESCHOOL

Best Practices in Action
Lesley Mandel Morrow and Linda B. Gambrell,
Series Editors

Connecting research findings to daily classroom practice is a key component of successful teaching—and any teacher can accomplish it, with the right tools. The Best Practices in Action series focuses on what elementary and middle grade teachers need to do "on Monday morning" to plan and implement high-quality literacy instruction and assess student learning. Books in the series are practical, accessible, and firmly grounded in research. Each title provides ready-to-use lesson ideas, engaging classroom vignettes, links to the Common Core State Standards, discussion questions and engagement activities ideal for professional learning communities, and reproducible materials that purchasers can download and print.

Teaching Informational Text in K–3 Classrooms:
Best Practices to Help Children Read, Write, and Learn
from Nonfiction
Mariam Jean Dreher and Sharon Benge Kletzien

Reading and Writing in Preschool:
Teaching the Essentials
Renée M. Casbergue and Dorothy S. Strickland

Oral Language and Comprehension in Preschool:
Teaching the Essentials
*Lesley Mandel Morrow, Kathleen A. Roskos,
and Linda B. Gambrell*

Oral Language and Comprehension in Preschool

Teaching the Essentials

Lesley Mandel Morrow
Kathleen A. Roskos
Linda B. Gambrell

Series Editors' Note by
Linda B. Gambrell and Lesley Mandel Morrow

THE GUILFORD PRESS
New York   London

Copyright © 2016 The Guilford Press
A Division of Guilford Publications, Inc.
370 Seventh Avenue, Suite 1200, New York, NY 10001
www.guilford.com

Printed in the United States of America

This book is printed on acid-free paper.

Last digit is print number: 9   8   7   6   5   4   3   2   1

Library of Congress Cataloging-in-Publication Data

Names: Morrow, Lesley Mandel, author. I Roskos, Kathy, author. I Gambrell,
   Linda B., author.
Title: Oral language and comprehension in preschool : teaching the essentials
   / Lesley Mandel Morrow, Kathleen A. Roskos, Linda B. Gambrell.
Description: New York : The Guilford Press, 2015. I Series: Best practices in
   action I Includes bibliographical references and index.
Identifiers: LCCN 2015042038I ISBN 9781462524006 (paperback) I ISBN
   9781462524129 (hardcover)
Subjects: LCSH: Language arts (Preschool) I English language—Study and
   teaching (Preschool). I BISAC: LANGUAGE ARTS & DISCIPLINES / Literacy. I
   EDUCATION / Preschool & Kindergarten.
Classification: LCC LB1140.5.L3 M665 2015 I DDC 372.6—dc23
LC record available at *http://lccn.loc.gov/2015042038*

Photo credits: Photos on pages 17, 81, and 120 by Getty. Photo on page 107
by Douglas H. Bushell

About the Authors

Lesley Mandel Morrow, PhD, is Distinguished Professor of Literacy and Director of the Center for Literacy Development at the Graduate School of Education at Rutgers, The State University of New Jersey. Her research, which she conducts with children and families from diverse backgrounds, deals with early literacy development and the organization and management of language arts programs and literacy-rich environments. Dr. Morrow has published more than 300 journal articles, chapters, and books. Her work has been recognized with awards including the Outstanding Teacher Educator in Reading Award and the William S. Gray Citation of Merit, both from the International Reading Association (IRA; now the International Literacy Association), and the Oscar S. Causey Award from the Literacy Research Association (LRA) for outstanding contributions to reading research. Dr. Morrow is past president of the IRA and is a member and past president of the Reading Hall of Fame.

Kathleen A. Roskos, PhD, is Professor in the Department of Education and School Psychology at John Carroll University, where she teaches courses in reading assessment and intervention. Formerly an elementary classroom teacher, Dr. Roskos has served in a variety of educational roles, including as director of federal programs in the public schools, department chair in higher education, director of the Ohio Literacy Initiative at the Ohio Department of Education, and a coprincipal investigator of several Early Reading First federal projects. Dr. Roskos studies early literacy development, teacher learning, and the instructional design of professional development for educators, and has published research articles, chapters, and books on these topics.

Linda B. Gambrell, PhD, is Distinguished Professor in the Eugene T. Moore School of Education at Clemson University. Her major research interests are in the areas of reading comprehension, literacy motivation, and the role of discussion in teaching and learning. She has published numerous books and articles on reading instruction, comprehension strategy instruction, and literacy motivation. She is a recipient of the Outstanding Teacher Educator in Reading Award from the IRA, the Albert J. Kingston Award from the LRA, the Laureate Award from the Association of Literacy Educators and Researchers (ALER), and, most recently, the Oscar S. Causey Award from the LRA. She is past president of the IRA, LRA, and ALER, and a member of the Reading Hall of Fame.

Series Editors' Note

A great deal of attention must focus on literacy development in early childhood. We know that young children have literacy skills, even though the literacy they demonstrate is not conventional. Emergent literacy behaviors have implications for instructional practice and later reading success. Like a child's first words and first steps, learning to read and write should be exciting and rewarding.

Currently there is a great deal of discussion about the importance of universal preschool in the United States. Research demonstrates the powerful effects that preschool has on a child's readiness for kindergarten and later literacy development. We also know that access to preschool is particularly important for children who are vulnerable. At a time when policymakers are beginning to notice the crucial role of preschool literacy development, it is essential to have good resources for educating and guiding preschool teachers that reinforce the following beliefs:

1. Teachers must be aware that children come to school with unique and varying degrees of prior knowledge about reading and writing and build on that knowledge.
2. Literacy learning requires a supportive positive school environment rich with accessible materials and varied experiences.
3. Teachers must serve as models for literacy behavior by scaffolding and demonstrating strategies to be learned.
4. During their literacy experiences, children should interact within a social context to share information and learn from one another.
5. Early reading and writing experiences are motivating when they are relevant and concrete; these activities should actively engage children.

6. Early reading and writing experiences need to provide systematic and explicit skill instruction.

7. A literacy development program should focus on experiences that integrate reading, writing, listening, speaking, and viewing within the language arts and in content areas such as music, art, social studies, science, and play.

8. Diversity in cultural and language backgrounds must be acknowledged and addressed in early literacy development.

9. Differences in literacy development will vary and are addressed with small-group and one-to-one differentiated instruction.

10. Assessment of achievement should be frequent and match instruction, and multiple formats for evaluating a student's literacy development should be used.

11. Standards for early literacy benchmarks should be tied to instruction and used as a means for reaching goals for all children to read fluently by the end of third grade.

12. Instruction must be age-appropriate for the development of children, with high and achievable expectations.

Literacy development must focus on both learning and teaching. Teachers must explicitly instruct children while also encouraging them to be actively involved in experiences where they can explore, experiment, and collaborate with others. Children must be motivated to view reading as a relevant act and to associate it with pleasure.

Oral Language and Comprehension in Preschool addresses two neglected but essential areas of development in early childhood. Children acquire language quite naturally based on the language they hear in their environment. However, for language to grow, intentional instruction is necessary. In the past, little emphasis was placed on comprehension in preschool. We know now that literacy development includes reading, listening, speaking, and viewing—and that reading entails not only the decoding of words but the comprehension of what is read or listened to.

This book provides a comprehensive look at oral language, listening, and comprehension development. The authors look at intentional, spontaneous, and incidental learning, and show concern for the preparation of a literacy-rich environment with books, charts, and labels throughout the room. They include measures of oral language and listening comprehension development, so teachers can plan instruction. Many strategies are presented to enhance and enrich oral language, and the needs of English language learners are considered. Play is also important for language development in preschool. Many activities are shared for the development of listening comprehension with storybook reading—discussing illustrations, authors, and types of books. When reading to children, a dialogic structure is essential. Children are asked to be storytellers and to participate in all types of story retelling. The book also explores ideas for encouraging parents to be partners in the literacy development of their children. At the end of each chapter, the authors share Ideas for Discussion, Reflection, and Action.

This book is designed to complement and be used with another book, *Reading and Writing in Preschool: Teaching the Essentials*, by Renée M. Casbergue and Dorothy S. Strickland. Both of these preschool books in our Best Practices in Action series draw on research, theory, policy, and practices that have proved successful in developing literacy. Both books take into account the joint position statement of the International Literacy Association (ILA) and the National Association for the Education of Young Children titled *Learning to Read and Write: Developmentally Appropriate Practices for Young Children* (1998), as well as the ILA's position statement *Literacy Development in the Preschool Years* (2006). They also consider the National Reading Panel Report (National Institute of Child Health and Human Development, 2000), the National Early Literacy Panel Report (National Center for Family Literacy, 2004), and the Common Core State Standards (National Governors Association Center for Best Practices & Council of Chief State School Officers, 2010).

Children come to school with diverse social, emotional, physical, and intellectual abilities and achievement levels. They have diverse cultural backgrounds, experiences, and exposures to literacy. Teachers must know how to address all these factors. The preschool books in our Best Practices in Action series embrace a comprehensive perspective toward literacy instruction by selecting the best techniques based on sound learning theories, such as a constructivist model or a problem-solving approach to more explicit instruction.

LINDA B. GAMBRELL, PhD
LESLEY MANDEL MORROW, PhD

REFERENCES

International Literacy Association. (2006). *Literacy development in the preschool years.* Newark, DE: Author.

International Literacy Association & National Association for the Education of Young Children. (1998). *Learning to read and write: Developmentally appropriate practices for young children.* Washington, DC: Author.

National Center for Family Literacy. (2004). *National Early Literacy Panel report.* Louisville, KY: Author.

National Governors Association Center for Best Practices & Council of Chief State School Officers. (2010). *Common Core State Standards.* Washington, DC: Author.

National Institute of Child Health and Human Development. (2000). *National Reading Panel report: Teaching children to read.* Washington, DC: Author

Preface

Children's language development is crucial to reading success. We can predict how successful a child is likely to be in school based on his or her language development from the age of 3. If a child is below level, he or she can overcome early deficits by attending a quality preschool. Years ago, conventional wisdom held that young children learn how to read, and later they read to learn. In fact, children must be involved in both activities early on. In addition to learning to read, children must learn what reading is for. That is, we read to learn and enjoy. Even in preschool, children can listen to someone read and then take part in sophisticated comprehension discussions about what was read.

Chapter 1 of this book deals with the importance of language and listening in the development of a reader. Oral language is the foundation of learning to read and write. Speaking and listening skills learned in the preschool years are crucial to future reading and writing achievement and school success. Children who do not develop sufficient oral language skills during this time find it difficult to keep pace with their peers in later years. They start to fall behind even before they start school (Biemiller, 2006; Dougherty, 2014; Hart & Risley, 2003; Scarborough, 2001; Snow, Burns, & Griffin, 1998).

Learning gaps that emerge early, however, can be overcome in preschools where there are language-rich contexts in which children are encouraged to talk, listen, and explore the concepts that words convey. Children need to learn how to carry on a good conversation with adults and peers. From age 3 onward, they should build a vocabulary store of at least 2,500 words per year (Biemiller & Slonim, 2001). They should encounter and practice using at least two to four new words each day. They need to learn how to attend and listen on purpose (Blair, 2002). They must set a steady pace toward meeting kindergarten entry expectations.

The key ideas in Chapter 1 include the need to (1) expand children's speaking and listening abilities and (2) layer the foundations for learning to read and write. Oral language includes five areas of knowledge and skill: semantics, syntax, morphology, phonology, and pragmatics. Oral language and literacy are alike in that they both deal with language as a way of representing the world. But they are also different because print requires extra mental work—to do more than say and listen to words, but also to read and write them. Oral language and literacy also share common skills (e.g., asking and answering questions). Comprehension of oral language is the ability to speak and listen with understanding. Children develop these skills through language experiences, substantive conversation, and oral language instruction. Oral language comprehension prepares the way for reading comprehension by increasing children's knowledge of language conventions, vocabulary, and listening comprehension. English language learners bring skills they used to learn their first language to learning a second language, but require more time and instruction to learn the sounds, words, and rules of the new language.

Chapter 2 discusses planning for talking, reading, and writing a lot. A quality early childhood program that integrates oral language and early literacy learning does not just happen. It takes planning, action, effective management, and attention to the continuous improvement of language and literacy instruction. Planning includes assessment that provides a clear picture of children's speaking, listening, reading, and writing abilities, and what they can accomplish in the short term and over the long term of a preschool program. It uses best practices to ensure that children are engaged and learning. It involves the effective use of resources, including time, materials, and other adults, to create the optimal supportive learning environment. Planning is the cornerstone of intentional teaching that helps children to make steady progress.

A major theme of this chapter is that early childhood settings where children talk, read, and write a lot are the result of thoughtful planning. Long-term planning involves goal setting using state-level early learning standards and/or the Head Start Child and Learning Development Framework (2010). Early childhood teachers should also be alert to the Common Core State Standards for English language arts (ELA) for kindergarten, and set children on a good pace to achieving these goals. A weekly planner works well for short-term planning where the teacher identifies weekly ELA objectives. Formative and summative assessments inform instructional planning. Teachers should plan for systematic formative assessment in their instruction. Various classroom-based assessments can be used for screening, progress monitoring, and evaluating children's development and growth in the language arts. When planning, teachers need to keep outcomes in mind for long-term units and day-to-day routines and rules. In spite of plans, teachers must remain flexible and responsive to the unexpected. Finally, teachers need to make the most of the resources they have (time, people, materials) to create a high-quality language and literacy environment for all the young children in the program.

In Chapter 3, we emphasize both setting up a rich literacy environment and strategies for promoting a rich literacy experience. Children in classrooms with literacy centers read and look at books much more often than children in classrooms without such collections. The efforts spent in creating an inviting atmosphere for classroom literacy centers are rewarded with increased interest in books (Guthrie, 2002; Gambrell, 2009; Wooten & Cullinan, 2009). The chapter also focuses on activities that integrate language, play, content, reading, and writing. As preschool educators, we hope to inspire children to become lifelong voluntary readers. When books are celebrated, young children are more likely to develop a positive attitude toward reading. In addition to read-alouds by the teacher, children need time to explore books and storytelling materials alone and with peers. With careful planning, teachers can help children make effective use of time and materials in literacy centers that foster a love of language, reading, and writing.

Chapter 4 discusses what effective preschools do to create supportive learning environments where preschoolers can work, play, and learn with understanding and joy. These steps are absolutely essential for ensuring children's oral language development and for establishing a permanent connection between oral language abilities and emerging early literacy skills. Children succeed when they are provided with learning conditions that nurture their language discoveries, their different uses of language, and their first attempts to read and write. When we create a supportive learning environment for talk, we also create opportunities for children to learn together about the real world. They also learn about possible worlds where they can discover the uses of their minds, imaginations, materials, and new technologies in a friendly community.

This chapter describes a number of teaching techniques and activities that nurture young children's language and conversational skills. In addition, key design elements for creating rich oral language environments are highlighted. Children thrive in learning environments that help them use what they already know to make sense of new information, help them build an understanding of acts and ideas, and help them check that their own thinking and actions are in line with the goals of an activity. A classroom environment that nurtures children's language and conversational skills is essential for ensuring oral language development and establishing a permanent connection between oral language abilities and emerging literacy skills.

Chapter 5 is titled "Developing Children's Listening Comprehension." The term *best practice* is generally used to describe those instructional approaches and techniques that have been demonstrated to improve children's learning. Best practices, in short, describe instructional methods that help children learn well. Evidence has shown that if these practices are used with fidelity, children are likely to become proficient in listening comprehension. The National Early Literacy Panel Report (2008) was perhaps the most ambitious effort to synthesize the literature in early reading, highlighting the key best practices in the field. This chapter describes several best practices specific to developing listening comprehension when using children's literature in the preschool classroom. These strategies play an important role in children's future reading achievement.

It is clear that there are many ways to enhance listening comprehension with young children. It is important that teachers select activities they know will develop comprehension. Stories need to be read in a dialogic manner, with discussion before reading to set a purpose and discussion after reading to encourage critical thinking or comprehension. We know it is important to repeat stories that have been read, and to read to both the entire class and to small groups. Storytelling is important since it is a tradition in so many cultures. If we immerse our students in literacy and purposely build listening with interactive discussions, the children will grow to enjoy literature and learn how to comprehend.

Chapter 6 discusses the role of the family in literacy development. We often forget how important families are to the development of literacy. A family is a child's first teacher and the teacher he or she will have longer than any others. When families provide a rich literacy environment at home, teaching reading and writing becomes easier for both the teacher and the child at school. Schools need to take responsibility for sharing information in the community about activities that families can implement at home before their children enter preschool and while they are in preschool. Teachers cannot be the only source of literacy in a child's life. Parents need to have books for their children at home and to read to them often. With home support, children can reach their full potential in literacy development.

In Chapter 7, we emphasize how literacy learning occurs within many learning situations. Many preschool classrooms follow an integrated school day, in which skills from all content areas are taught within the context of a topic of study. In an interdisciplinary approach, topics are drawn from children's interests and experiences. Learning experiences are socially interactive and process oriented, giving children time to explore and experiment.

Good teaching takes a great deal of planning. Children need a daily routine they can count on. They also need to be engaged in relevant and meaningful activities. Themes help to make the curriculum both relevant and meaningful. Embedding literacy throughout the school day, when doing science, social studies, math, art, music, and play, is advisable because literacy development is of the utmost importance throughout preschool. Teachers need to stay on top of the past, the present, and new ideas. Professional development is necessary to enhance teaching methods. This chapter includes a detailed look at a day in one exemplary preschool classroom. The purpose is to show how teachers can bring language and literacy to life for preschool children.

Contents

4. Nurturing Young Children's Language and Conversational Skills   62

5. Developing Children's Listening Comprehension   80

6. Reading with Children at Home   107

CHAPTER I

The Importance of Speaking and Listening in Early Literacy

In Ms. Rivero's preschool class, the children are well along in their exploration of health and exercise. They have learned the names of major muscles (e.g., biceps) and exercised their muscles to make them stronger. They also encountered the word *skeleton* in connection with their bodies. They examined the photo of a human skeleton, compared human and animal skeletons, and even explored a three-dimensional human skeleton online. Quite fascinated by this part of his body, Jaquan (kindergarten ready), motions for Ms. Judy, the preschool director, to come over by him. He leans in close to her and whispers as he points to his chest, "All my bones

in there . . . All of 'em . . . from here [points to his head] to here [points to his toes] is my skeleton. My skel-l-l-e-ton." Then, in a very hushed tone, "It's not scary!"

THE ENGLISH LANGUAGE ARTS IN PRESCHOOL

Speaking, listening, reading, and writing are collectively referred to as the English language arts (ELA). Each domain is indeed an *art* that requires considerable knowledge and skill for effective use in school and in life. In a global society, developing young children's language arts abilities is essential for their active participation in an increasingly online world.

Speaking and listening combine to form the oral language side of the ELA, and reading and writing represent its written language side. Oral language is also referred to as *orality*. Written language is termed *literacy*. Oral language and written language are interactive; they are in a reciprocal relationship with each other. This is to say that oral language informs written language, and written language influences oral language. When 4-year-old Henry shouts, "I pounce like a panther!" for example, he uses words from the e-book *Fierce Grey Mouse* (Bourgonje, 2013) that he recently read with his dad to describe what he is doing.

Oral language is the foundation of learning to read and write. Speaking and listening skills learned in the preschool years are crucial to future reading and writing achievement and school success. Children who do not develop sufficient oral language skills during this time find it difficult to keep pace with their peers in later years. They start to fall behind even before they start school (Biemiller, 2006; Dougherty, 2014; Hart & Risley, 2003; Scarborough, 2001; Snow, Burns, & Griffin, 1998).

Learning gaps that emerge early, however, can be overcome in language-rich contexts where children are encouraged to talk, listen, and explore the concepts that words convey. As the vignette from Ms. Rivero's class illustrates, preschoolers are fascinated with words, like the word *skeleton* in a study of health and fitness. In the process of learning about the word *skeleton*, these preschoolers also explored related words like *rib cage*, *elbow*, *backbone*, and *tibia* (especially *tibia*, because it even sounds like a hard word). One word, in short, led to another, creating a language-rich learning environment.

In sum, children need to learn to use language a lot in the preschool years. They need to learn how to carry on a good conversation with adults and peers. From age 3 onward, they should build a vocabulary store of at least 2,500 words per year (Biemiller & Slonim, 2001). They should encounter and practice using at least two to four new words each day. They need to learn how to attend and listen on purpose (Blair, 2002). They must set a steady pace toward meeting kindergarten-entry expectations. All together, preschoolers should steadily develop and improve skills in the following oral language areas:

1. *Semantics*: Developing meanings for the words they hear and say in their conversations with others.
2. *Syntax* (also known as grammar): Learning the rules of how words are linked together.
3. *Morphology*: Figuring out how to manipulate the smallest units of meaning in the language called morphemes. The word *preschool*, for example, has two morphemes: *pre* (meaning before) and *school*.
4. *Phonology*: Understanding the sound structure of language. From birth onward (or even before) children are learning all the sounds or phonemes of their language.
5. *Pragmatics*: Understanding the social uses of language and basic social rules like saying "hello" and "good-bye," saying "please" and "thank you," and taking turns in a conversation.

With adults' help, most children rapidly develop their oral language skills in these areas before they go to school, and together these skills form the oral language foundation for learning to read and write at school. This is true in any language system, not just English. All languages start with a group of sounds that must be learned and used by the infants in the families that speak that language. All languages have words that are made up of a variety of those sounds, and all conversation in all languages is made up of a group of words put together to express an idea. Communication in any language involves expressing and receiving ideas in a way that is understandable for all the people involved in the communication.

For young children who come from homes where English is not the primary language, all of these skills will have been developed in their home language. They will have learned the sounds of their language, the words of their language, and how to put words together to form ideas. So these young children will already know a great deal about how language works. They will bring those skills to the task of learning a new language; but it is important to remember that these children will need to start again with the sounds and the words of their new language, and with the rules about how conversation works in this language.

THE ORAL LANGUAGE–EARLY LITERACY RELATIONSHIP

Before children are readers and writers, they are speakers and listeners. Progressing from saying words to reading and writing them demands an intellectual shift in children's thinking. They must become conceptually aware that there is a code to be deciphered and that it is different from speech. Reading print is more than understanding speech written down. The following concepts explain how oral language and literacy are both alike and different. Two exceptions apply: (1) not all languages have a written form, and (2) some languages that are written do not use an alphabet or do not have an alphabet that is composed of 26 letters.

Concept 1: Talk and Print Are Alike

Talking, reading, and writing are interrelated processes. All three involve using words to *stand for* or represent persons, objects, and events in the world. Each draws from the other in real experience. Children speak and listen, they listen to reading, they read what they write, and so on. These overlapping processes are what Vygotsky (1962) described as "tools of the mind" that children can use to get things done. Talking, reading, and writing join together to build children's knowledge about the world and about words. At the starting line of learning to read and write, children rely on their considerable speech experiences to help them with print experiences.

Concept 2: Talk and Print Are Different

There are important differences between spoken and written language that make learning to read harder than learning to talk. Why? There are two main reasons. First, print is a code for speech that relies on the manipulation of a set of symbols (26 alphabet letters), and because it is a code, children need to be taught how to decode print before they can say it. This extra step requires extra mental effort. Adults must help children find the relationship between print symbols and speech sounds and help them make the effort to remember. Second, print is decontextualized: It does not have the real-time qualities of speech, such as tone, pitch, expression, and rhythm, that signal meaning. Before they go to school, children experience mostly talking that occurs in rich contexts. When a mother says to her 4-year-old son, "Put on your pajamas. It's time for bed," there are real environment cues to help him know what this means. Children also interact with peers in rich, meaningful, social play situations that provide many signals about what to say and do. Even speech on television and computer games has many sensory clues as to what the talk refers to and why a person is talking.

Print is different. It is silent and still. Meaning must be unbundled from the print itself by an active mind. This, too, requires extra mental effort to pick out the meaning from the words alone. Adults must show children how to think with print to make it meaningful. This is why reading to and with children is so powerful—because it shows them how to do what they need to do to comprehend the print code.

Concept 3: Speaking, Listening, Reading, and Writing Share Skills

Fortunately, skills learned for oral language are shared with literacy and vice versa. A few of the most essential skills are making predictions, asking and answering questions, telling and retelling, sense of story, and phonological awareness. You can think of these as *crossover skills* because they are used in children's talking, reading, and writing to the benefit of all three. Each skill leads to more complex skills that strengthen and enrich children's abilities to use the language arts in more challenging learning experiences. Knowing how to teach these skills will help you be more effective and efficient as you plan language experiences for the active talkers and emerging readers and writers in your setting.

Making Predictions

This is the ability to use context to choose the appropriate language. At a friend's birthday party, children remember to say "happy birthday" because the setting reminds them of the event. As a familiar bedtime favorite, they can chime in, chanting "Chicka, chicka, boom, boom" as you read aloud the storybook to them. Similarly, they use the skill of prediction to guess what a printed word might be when they hear its beginning sound or connect visual cues with the meaning (e.g., the tail-like form of the letter *g* at the end of the word *pig*).

Asking and Answering Questions

In oral language, questions are signs of seeking, noticing, and incorporating new and more complex experiences into prior experiences. They signal what's going on in children's minds while mental schemas are being organized and built. Questions indicate children's skill in monitoring comprehension; through their questions, we can see that children are "following along" and "getting it," whether it be a conversation, a book reading, a play episode, or a table activity. Questioning is a vital skill in speaking and listening as well as in reading and writing.

Telling and Retelling

These expressive verbal skills exercise children's use of language to tell, recount, report, explain, and pretend. Children need many opportunities to practice their expressive language skills so that they learn to include the details. In speaking, listening, reading, and writing, details matter. Attention to detail increases the length of sentences, the size of vocabulary, and the grammatical complexity of the talk. Details also enlarge the child's store of background knowledge.

Sense of Story

Children's personal stories about their real experiences indicate their storytelling abilities. Stories are one way they learn to represent their experience. Stories provide an organizer for holding an experience in mind and replaying it at will. Storytelling is also the forerunner of grasping the story structures found in literature. Children's oral storytelling abilities lay the foundation for using story elements to comprehend stories in books.

Phonological Awareness

As a skill, phonological awareness places special demands on children's abilities to self-regulate their thinking and actions. They must listen for specific words or sounds; listen to words and sounds carefully to manipulate them; and listen with the intention to act for a specific purpose, such as clapping for each word heard in a sentence, tapping for each sound heard in a word, completing a rhyme, singing and clapping in rhythm, and so on. Learning to read and write depends heavily on phonemic awareness, which is the basis of matching sounds to printed letters and decoding printed words.

Table 1.1 summarizes how oral language and literacy are alike and how they are different. Compare and contrast Halliday's functions of language and five functions of early literacy (Neuman & Roskos, 1989). Note how the functions or uses of language and literacy overlap. Both, for example, are means for interacting with others. However, their uses also differ in important ways. Literacy, for example, is used for exploring the world through print (signs), whereas language is used to explore the world through oral exchanges. To become literate, young children need writing to help them learn about reading, they need reading to help them learn about writing, and they need oral language to help them learn about both. When you are knowledgeable about the relationship between talk and print you can help young children make the mental shift from the more familiar world of talking to the less familiar one of reading and writing.

ORAL LANGUAGE COMPREHENSION

Oral language comprehension is the ability to speak and listen with understanding. It is that part of the Common Core State Standards for English Language Arts and Literacy (CCSS-ELA; National Governors Association Center for Best Practices & Council of Chief State School Officers [NGA & CCSSO], 2010) that addresses the communication areas of speaking, listening, and language. It involves

TABLE 1.1. Compare and Contrast Oral Language and Literacy

Language	Literacy
Instrumental: *I want.*	Exploratory: *How does it work?*
Regulatory: *Do as I say.*	Interactional: *Between you and me.*
Interactional: *You and me.*	Personal: *For me.*
Personal: *Here I come.*	Authenticating: *To legitimate.*
Heuristic: *Tell me why.*	Transactional: *Between me and text.*
Imaginative: *Let's pretend.*	

the strategies and skills of comprehension and collaboration (e.g., participating in collaborative conversations about grade-level topics and texts), the presentation of knowledge and ideas (e.g., describing people, places, things, and events with relevant details), and effective use of conventions, language, and vocabulary. It is the bedrock of future reading comprehension, broadly defined as the ability to read with understanding.

Oral language comprehension provides the evidence of a child's oral language development. When 4-year-old Josie actively listens and takes turns in a conversation about a family trip, for example, she demonstrates how far she has come in her own oral language development. In this respect, oral language comprehension involves the primary areas of language development described above: semantics, syntax, morphology, phonology, and pragmatics.

Oral language comprehension is *more than the sum* of these parts. Oral language comprehension requires the *integration* of all oral language areas in order to speak and to listen with intention and purpose. The child must not only develop specific skills in each of these primary areas (e.g., syntax), but also know how to combine this linguistic information across them all to produce meaningful talk and listening.

Children develop their oral language comprehension in many ways—but three opportunities are key: (1) language experiences, (2) substantive conversation, and (3) oral language instruction. You will learn more about each in the following chapters, along with best practices that ensure all children have access to these opportunities at home and at school.

Language Experience

Language experience involves all those real-life experiences that are powerful motivators of language use, like Lucy's account of her tonsil operation: "I had some purple juice that made me asleep and I didn't feel it. Had this big ange [bandage] here sticking on my arm. And they had to sew it together." Such accounts can readily be turned into dictated language experience stories at school for sharing and repeated reading.

Substantive Conversation

Substantive conversation is a form of talk between adults and children that informs, explains, and elaborates on ideas. It often includes teachable moments, when adults have the opportunity to provide background knowledge on topics. It involves expanding the amount of child talk in a conversation and stretching the conversation to add details, new words, and new language structures, such as adjectives and adverbs, idioms, and figurative language. Consider this example between father and daughter while reading *One Morning in Maine* by Robert McCloskey (1976).

HEATHER: Are those the trees that they're talking about?

FATHER: Yeah, those are pine trees.

HEATHER: We have pine trees out back.

FATHER: We have some, but not so many, do we?

HEATHER: Yeah.

FATHER: Remember there were so many in Maine. Sometimes when the fog came up we couldn't see them, remember that? Real gray and foggy. Then when the fog went away we saw all little islands filled with trees just like that.

Oral Language Instruction

Oral language instruction is a teaching and learning context that can be used to instruct children about language and how to effectively use their speaking and listening skills. Adults nurture children's oral language comprehension when they set out to intentionally teach them something. Children's lives are replete with these instructional episodes that range from very short interactions (e.g., explaining an idea or how to do something) to more extended ones (e.g., shared book reading). When Henry's mother teaches him how to tie his shoe, for example, she uses talk and action in a way that pins Henry's attention to the activity (he listens on purpose) and asks him to use words as tools for remembering ("Step 1: Cross the laces like normal" and so on). When teachers engage children in shared book reading discussions (which they should do often), they also provide opportunities for children to practice and strengthen their oral language comprehension.

ORAL LANGUAGE COMPREHENSION LEADS
TO READING COMPREHENSION

To be a participating member in conversations at home and school depends on effective oral language comprehension skills. As the ability to speak and listen with understanding improves, children learn more and more oral language skills from an ever-widening world of social and academic situations. They learn, in short, by speaking, listening, and using language, and therefore develop their own oral language comprehension prowess.

Oral language comprehension skills are essential for communication, but they are equally critical for written communication. In achieving early literacy, young children need writing to help them learn about reading, they need reading to help them learn about writing, and they need oral language comprehension to help them learn about both.

For purposes of early literacy learning, the concepts and skills of oral language comprehension can be organized into three large skill domains: language conventions, vocabulary, and listening comprehension. Each domain is further described below, emphasizing those skills that have a strong bearing on early literacy skills, such as print awareness and story comprehension. High-quality oral language comprehension instruction for children in general equally applies to those children for whom English is a second language and those with special needs (Dixon et al., 2012; Goldenberg, 2008).

Language Conventions

In his classic text *The Foundations of Literacy*, Don Holdaway (1979, p. 62) describes the important language factors that link to early literacy as "familiarity with written dialect in oral form." What he meant by this was that as children gain familiarity with book language, through being read to, they begin to incorporate it into their own talk—terms like *clever indeed! Once upon a time*, *It seems a pity*, and *First, next, . . . then*. This is the kind of language usage that prepares children for learning to read and write.

Subsequent research summaries of early literacy predictors corroborate the role of oral language, specifically grammar and usage, in preparing children for the learn-to-read process (Snow, Burns, & Griffin, 1998; Whitehurst & Lonigan, 1998). It is not just any talk that builds bridges to early literacy. Rather it is talk that involves (1) more complex grammatical structures, such as contractions (*I'm, we're, they're*) and pronouns (*she, he, they, it*); (2) structures that imply consequence, comparison, and temporal order (*if . . . then, because . . . like and different . . . first, next . . .*); and (3) intonation patterns (*Once upon a time and way long ago there was a princess who lived on a glass hill*) and terms (*however, therefore*) that are nonconversational in form that build bridges to the written discourse of books. Children benefit from a language environment that provides many opportunities for them to expand their grammatical awareness and the usage of compound and complex sentences they eventually will be required to read. Strategies that help to support English language learners include (1) slow but natural levels of speech; (2) clear enunciation; (3) short, simple sentences; (4) repetition and paraphrasing; and (5) controlled vocabulary and idioms.

Vocabulary

Our vocabulary consists of those words we know, love, and use. Lately, the 4-year-olds in Ms. Starr's Head Start classroom, for example, simply love the word *swooped* and use it every chance they get, as in "I sw-o-o-o-o-ped in to grab my milk!"

Vocabulary knowledge is that body of words known by a person. It is organized into two kinds: receptive and expressive vocabulary. Receptive vocabulary consists of words *known by association* when listening or reading. For example, when Ella Mae hears her mother read that Peter Rabbit was a *naughty* little rabbit, she understands the word by associating it with Peter's misdeeds in Mr. McGregor's garden. Word meaning, in brief, is understood in the context of hearing it or reading it.

Expressive vocabulary consists of those words we can produce or those *known by person*. The person can produce the word as needed to fit the circumstances. This time, when reading the story, Ella Mae points to Peter Rabbit and says he *wiggled* under the fence. She retrieves the word from her own memory.

In young children, their receptive vocabulary is typically larger than their expressive vocabulary, as we might expect. They can hear and understand more words than they can necessarily say and use in different situations.

The significance of vocabulary knowledge in the early years for future learning is profound. By age 3, children already show large differences in vocabulary that persist through high school and perpetuate ever-widening achievement gaps. Vocabulary knowledge at age 3, in fact, predicts reading comprehension at grade three (Hart & Risley, 2003; Stanovich, 1986). Children with poor vocabulary at an early age are less likely to learn words incidentally (Robbins & Ehri, 1994) and typically have less background knowledge for oral language comprehension, which in turn impacts their early literacy development (Hirsch, 2006; Neuman & Wright, 2014). Upon entry to kindergarten, low-vocabulary children already have far fewer word meanings than their average and above-average peers. By the end of second grade this number swells to 2,000 fewer word meanings than their peers, which puts them seriously at risk for acquiring the 6,000 word meanings they need for third grade reading comprehension (Biemiller, 2010). To prevent falling further behind in the primary grades, low-vocabulary preschoolers need plenty of rich oral language activities—as well as direct instruction by adults—to build up their store of word meanings at kindergarten entry.

Children's vocabulary knowledge (store of word meanings or lexicon) also impacts their acquisition of decoding skills, providing linguistic information (e.g., phoneme awareness) for mapping spoken language to print (Ehri, 2014; Wagner et al., 1997). Word meanings help children with word reading (Perfetti & Stafura, 2014). Meanings supply cues for identifying *and* comprehending words, which develops the word-to-text skills children need for comprehension. Vocabulary is the link between word-reading skills and comprehension processes. The size and quality of children's vocabulary knowledge (word meanings or lexicon), therefore, has serious consequences for children's school readiness in general and their overall literacy development (National Early Literacy Panel [NELP], 2008).

Adults can ensure that young children acquire the vocabulary they need for reading achievement by using teaching strategies that range from incidental, or happenstance, to more intentional, or deliberate instruction.

Traditionally, early childhood teachers have used incidental strategies to help children learn new words, capitalizing on *teachable moments* in the course of everyday routines and learning activities. While spontaneous, these strategies can nonetheless be quite powerful for several reasons.

1. Adult talk is geared to the goals of activity, or goal oriented.
2. Adult talk is contingent on the child's talk, that is, dependent on the child's understanding at the moment.
3. It provides immediate feedback to the child, which is impactful.

Study the examples provided in Table 1.2 and note these important features of incidental strategies. When present and of high quality, they can provide rich opportunities that help children learn new words.

Recent research shows the benefits of intentional strategies for strengthening vocabulary knowledge, especially for children with vocabulary delays (Marulis

TABLE 1.2. Incidental Strategies

Incidental strategy	Example
Carrying on conversation	CHILD: What's a *pleat*?
	TEACHER: That's an interesting word. What do you think it is?
	CHILD: A skirt.
	TEACHER: Oh . . . someone talked to you about a pleated skirt. Well . . . the pleat is a fold of cloth in the skirt. When you spin around the pleats spread apart, and the skirt sort of lifts up.
	CHILD: Oh . . . like an umbrella.
Explaining terms in the course of events	CHILD: Ms. E. said it was hot in here and that made the water vaporate, and that vaporation makes flowers droop.
	MS. E.: Yes, water evaporates from the soil when it's hot, and then the plant doesn't have enough water. It wilts or droops.
Promoting vocabulary in storybook reading	Finally he encountered a "big thing" (*Are You My Mother?* by P. D. Eastman, 1998).
	CHILD: It's not his mother.
	TEACHER: It's not his mother? What does it look like?
	CHILD: Like a toy.
	TEACHER: You've seen a toy like that?
	CHILD: It's a dump truck.
	TEACHER: It's something that lifts up dirt in a big shovel.
	CHILD: It's a crane.
	TEACHER: Yes, like a crane.

& Neuman, 2010). Intentional strategies use direct, intensive adult language to deliberately teach new words. Several promising strategies have emerged. Silverman (2007), for example, describes anchored vocabulary instruction that combines oral contextual strategies (e.g., linking new words to personal experience) and analytical strategies (e.g., attending to letters and sounds of new words) that bridge oral and print sources of word meanings. More direct, Biemiller and Boote (2006) found that well-placed vocabulary *interruptions* to explain word meanings in a repeated readings approach boosted kindergarteners' vocabulary knowledge. In this approach, target words are selected from a storybook or informational text. The text is read two times: first without interruption and then with periodic interruptions to explain a few target word meanings. The teacher says the target word, points out its form (letter and sound features), and uses it in context. He or she then asks the students to say the word, use it in a sentence, and say it again. This technique yielded sufficient word learning gains to justify instructional time spent. Similarly, Smeets and Bus (2012) found that multiple-choice questions embedded in an interactive electronic storybook either during or after reading increased word learning measurably over incidental comments and even dictionary hot spots in storybook reading. Here—as the child reads the e-book—the story periodically "pauses" on a screen page where the young reader is prompted to answer a question about a word meaning by clicking on a picture. A lovable virtual tutor (a small, fuzzy creature) says, for example, "Time for a question. Bear is *shy*. Where can you see that?" Three pictures are displayed and the child is asked to click on a choice; the tutor provides immediate feedback to the response. The enhanced e-book proved to be as effective in helping children learn word meanings as adult explanations.

Instructional features common across these intentional strategies include (1) a before–during–after (BDA) instructional framework to introduce, discuss, and review new words; (2) repetition and explanation of new words in context (e.g., of a storybook); and (3) plenty of opportunities to practice using new words in a variety of settings. The goal in all is to provide purposeful exposure to new words, including high-utility root words and disciplinary content words.

Listening Comprehension

Listening comprehension starts to develop early in life, around age 1, and continues to grow during the elementary school years. It involves oral language competencies, such as the ability to parse the speech stream (talk) into morpheme and syntactic units, vocabulary, sentence structures, and anaphoric referents (referring back to prior statements and ideas in conversation) among other skills (e.g., background knowledge; Samuels, 1987).

During the preschool and primary grades, children's listening comprehension *leads* their reading comprehension. This is to say that their listening comprehension predicts their reading achievement. Children with advanced listening comprehension prior to kindergarten are about a year ahead of their average peers, whereas those with delays are about a year behind. While competencies increase for all children, the gap widens across the elementary school years. By grade three, advanced children's listening comprehension is equivalent to that of average children in grade four, while slower-progressing children are similar to average second graders or even younger children.

Broadly speaking, young children's listening comprehension can only increase through interactions with others and with books that introduce new vocabulary, concepts, and language structures. Because they cannot yet read, most of children's listening skill growth comes from nonprint sources such as talk, media, play, and adult read-alouds. And for many children this continues to be the case throughout the elementary grade years (Biemiller, 2003).

For this fundamental reason (listening leads reading), children need a full menu of oral language activities that helps them learn to use listening as a tool for meaningful (and memorable) comprehension. Activities that ask children to respond to direct questions; talk and listen in small groups; question to clarify or gain further information; recount events; and respond to stories, songs, and poems are key. When children are guided to listen with intention and purpose (attentively), they can participate more fully in conversations and in turn gain more from high-quality social and instructional interactions that build a solid foundation for reading and writing.

CONCLUSION

Several key ideas conclude this chapter. From the start it is important to understand that speaking, listening, reading, and writing comprise the ELA. In preschool, the ELA focus is on oral language with the twofold goal of (1) expanding children's speaking and listening abilities and (2) laying the foundations for learning to read and write. Oral language includes five areas of knowledge and skill: semantics, syntax, morphology, phonology, and pragmatics. Oral language and literacy are alike in that they both deal with language as a way of representing the world. But they are also different because print requires extra mental work to do more than say and listen to words, but also to read and write them. Oral language and literacy also share common skills (e.g., asking and answering questions). Oral language comprehension is the ability to speak and listen with understanding. Children develop it through language experiences, substantive conversation, and oral language instruction. Oral language comprehension prepares the way for reading comprehension by increasing children's knowledge and skill with language conventions, vocabulary, and listening comprehension. English language learners bring the skills they use to learn their first language to learning a second language, but will require more time and instruction to learn the sounds, words, and conversation rules of the new one.

Preschool in Practice

Personalizing Professional Development

The teachers at Hopkins Early Childhood Center value their own professional learning. Finding time to learn, however, can be challenging in the busy, bustling world of teaching young children. But these teachers have found the time by taking advantage of online resources and tech tools that are so readily available these days.

Currently several PreK teachers are enrolled in an online module offered free of charge through their local educational services center. The module is entitled *Language for Learning in the Early Years* (Roskos, 2008), and addresses the following professional learning goals:

- Understand the major domains of oral language development.
- Examine approaches that support oral language learning.
- Distinguish key elements of supportive approaches.
- Plan to use supportive approaches in classroom practice.

The module provides teachers with background on the essentials of oral language development and learning. It offers concrete examples of how to support children's developing oral language skills. And it aligns with the Language Modeling domain of the Classroom Assessment Scoring System (CLASS; Pianta, LaParo, & Hamre, 2008), which is used at the center for the evaluation of teaching skills. The module's multimedia and interactive format is also very engaging. Best of all, individual teachers can view the module based on their personal schedules and at their own pace.

The teachers like the option of online modules as a way to personalize their own professional development. Digital pioneers, several Hopkins teachers also use Twitter to connect with fellow educators on common topics and issues, such as technology in the preschool classroom. They like the fact that they can pose questions and get answers almost immediately. Others like to participate in webinars and blogs (e.g., *www.ernweb.com*) that help them keep up to date and learn from others. The most recent webinar on creating high-impact literacy stations for PreK children was a big hit!

At Hopkins, teachers are effectively using social media and online offerings in combination within their professional learning community to develop their own personalized professional development plans and reflect on how that professional development is affecting the teaching they do every day.

Aligning ELA Standards

The CCSS-ELA framework is an aligned set of standards across grades K–12. It maps end-of-year expectations for knowledge and skills in reading, writing, speaking, listening, and language. The PreK teachers at Garrison Elementary School recognize the importance of aligning the statewide early learning standards in the language arts to the kindergarten CCSS-ELA expectations. They want to make sure that the language and literacy expectations for their kindergarten-bound students start them well on their way to meeting kindergarten expectations down the road—and that there are no major instructional gaps in the PreK language and literacy program.

To complete the alignment task, they carved out time at their regular grade-level meetings in the fall. Working together, they "mapped" each early learning standard in the state language and literacy domains to one or more standards in the kindergarten CCSS-ELA set. Several examples from the Reading Foundations map are provided in Table 1.3. Although the alignment task took considerable time, it was worth it. The teachers found two large gaps in their language and literacy program that needed to be addressed: developing emergent reader skills with those children who appeared ready, and exploring digital tools to produce and publish early writing. They used this information to (1) plan small-group instructional activities in emergent reading skills for high letter-knowledge children (e.g., sound-stretching words to map phonemes to letters, modeling use of the word wall for writing and reading level A texts), and (2) adding iPads to the writing center and showing children how to use age-appropriate apps (e.g., Doodle Buddy from Pinger, Inc., available through iTunes: *https://itunes. apple.com/us/app/doodle-buddy-paint-draw-scribble/id313232441?mt=8*) for creating drawings and stories together and on their own.

CHILDREN'S LITERATURE CITED IN THIS CHAPTER

Are You My Mother? by P. D. Eastman (1998). Random House.
Fierce Grey Mouse by Chantal Bourgonje (2013). Tizio.
One Morning in Maine by Robert McCloskey (1976). Puffin Books.

TABLE 1.3. Aligning Statewide Early Learning Standards to the CCSS-ELA for Kindergarten

ELDS–Early Reading	CCSS–Reading Kindergarten
Ask and answer questions, and comment about characters and major events in familiar stories.	RL.K.1
ELDS–Print Concepts	
Demonstrate an understanding of basic conventions of print in English and other languages.	RF.K.1
ELDS–Phonological Awareness	
With modeling and support, recognize and produce rhyming words.	RF.K.2.a

Note. ELDS, Early Learning and Development Standards (Ohio).

IDEAS FOR DISCUSSION, REFLECTION, AND ACTION

1. Record the language of two or three preschoolers engaged in a similar activity at the sand table, in dramatic play, or in a joint project. Transcribe and analyze a 5- to 8-minute portion of the language sample. Note the children's use of vocabulary, grammar, sentence complexity, and pragmatics. Share your observations with a peer who has also collected a language sample. What are the similarities? What are the differences?

2. In this chapter, both spontaneous incidental learning and intention instruction are discussed. Describe the differences between the two types of learning situations and give an example of each.

3. In the discussion of oral language in this chapter, we learn that there are five areas of knowledge and skill for a child to learn: semantics, syntax, morphology, phonology, and pragmatics. Define each term and provide descriptions of how children are engaged in learning these elements in spontaneous ways with family and in preschool.

4. At the end of this chapter, some Early Learning Development Standards are compared with the CCSS. The CCSS do not have a preschool section. Study the CCSS for kindergarten for Reading Literature and Reading Informational Text. Describe if and how these can be used in preschool but in a more appropriate manner for 3- and 4-year-olds.

CHAPTER 2

Planning for Talking, Reading, and Writing a Lot

Ms. Campbell's Head Start class is deeply engaged in a study of pipes and pumps. They collected a variety of pipes for display in their plumbing shop. They watched a video about pipes from Home Depot, and learned that PVC pipe is made of plastic, not copper, which is a metal. They tested water flow with different-sized pipes from tiny (½ inch) to large (2 inch) and studied how a pump works. After several pipe/pump walks through their school building, they decide to make dioramas of the pipes and pumps they find in their own homes. Describing a diorama that he made with his friends, Anthony points to a tiny plastic spider by an aluminum foil pipe in the display and reports, "We see-ed spiders in our basements. James see-ed a really *big* one by the pipe, but it runned away. . . ."

A quality early childhood program that integrates oral language and early literacy learning does not just happen. It takes planning, action, effective management, and attention to the continuous improvement of language and literacy instruction. Planning includes assessment that provides a clear picture of children's speaking, listening, reading, and writing abilities, and what they can accomplish in the short term and over the long term of your program. It uses best practices to ensure that children are engaged and learning. It involves the effective use of resources, including time, materials, and other adults, to create the optimal supportive learning environment. Planning is the cornerstone of intentional teaching that helps children make steady progress.

LONG-TERM PLANNING

Long-term planning describes the learning aims for children's oral language and early literacy over the entire time of your program year. To plan effectively, you need to be familiar with academic content standards in the ELA that define the speaking, listening, reading, and writing abilities for preschoolers and kindergarteners. You not only need to know the ELA knowledge and skills expected of preschoolers that prepare them for kindergarten, but also those of kindergarteners down the road to ensure continuity in language and literacy development.

Early childhood teachers are guided by two primary sources of academic standards in ELA: (1) the Head Start Child and Learning Development Framework (2010), and/or (2) state-level early learning standards. The content for standards (what children need to know and be able to do) comes from both scholarly research and professional wisdom. Children's oral language development has been a topic of intense study for decades, and much has been learned as to when and how speech and language develops in early childhood (e.g., Bloom, 2002). Likewise how early literacy develops has benefited from a fairly large body of research, albeit over a shorter period of time. Not long ago, the NELP (2008) produced an extensive synthesis of the scientific research on early literacy, which identified the skills and concepts young children need to learn to succeed as readers and writers, and the instructional practices that enhance early literacy learning. Key predictors of reading and writing success include alphabet knowledge, phonological awareness, rapid automatic naming of letters and numbers, ability to write one's own name, and phonological memory. Instruction designed to teach children letter–sound relationships in combination with shared book reading was found to have large positive effects on young children's early literacy learning. Standards makers use these scholarly sources to ground their decisions about expectations. Where research has not yet converged on clear evidence as to *what children should know when*, early childhood educators draw on their own reasoning informed by teaching practice to make judgments about language and literacy milestones. Their *informed opinion* also supports what content to include in standards.

The Head Start Child and Learning Development Framework (2010) promotes and defines positive outcomes in early childhood programs serving children 3–5 years old. It describes the developmental building blocks found essential for learning at school and in life. Specific to the ELA, the Framework includes three domains: the Language Development and Literacy Knowledge & Skills domains apply to all young children, whereas the English Language Development domain applies only to dual-language learners. Each domain consists of elements and examples of those elements. The Language Development domain, for example, addresses receptive language, that is, the ability to comprehend or understand language, and expressive language, or the ability to use language. Evidence that a young child *comprehends increasingly complex and varied vocabulary*, for instance, is an example (or indicator) of receptive language ability. The complete set of domain elements and examples in the ELA can be accessed on the Head Start website (*http://eclkc.ohs.acf.hhs.gov/hslc/tta-system/teaching/eecd/assessment/child%20outcomes/revised-child-outcomes.html*).

Today, all states have developed early learning standards for PreK-age children, which can be accessed at each state's Department of Education website. Ohio's *Early Learning and Development Standards in Language and Literacy Development*, for example, span birth to age 5 and consist of three strands (Listening and Speaking, Reading, Writing). Each strand includes topics (e.g., *Early Reading*) with specific indicators (e.g., *Actively participate in book reading, story telling, and singing*). Many states that use the CCSS have aligned their early learning standards to the kindergarten-level CCSS-ELA standards. California is one state that has completed this process. Listening and speaking skills developed at the preschool level, such as vocabulary, are keyed to Vocabulary Acquisition and Use standards in the CCSS-ELA. (See publication available at *www.cde.ca.gov/sp/cd/re/psalignment.asp*.)

In a nutshell, ELA standards describe what we can (and should) expect from children as they grow and develop as speakers, listeners, readers, and writers in the early years. Increasingly, early childhood professionals view children's language and literacy development along a continuum of knowledge and skills from birth to age 8, which not only prepares children for kindergarten but also for literacy success in grade 3. From this 21st-century perspective, it is critical that early childhood teachers know and regularly use preschool and kindergarten ELA standards to guide their planning for language and literacy instruction. For the English language learners in your classroom, look carefully for state-level and professional information about how these standards should be applied to them.

SHORT-TERM PLANNING

Standards help us to achieve consensus about what children should know and be able to do in the language arts. We can all agree, for example, that children should use an increasingly complex and varied vocabulary across the preschool years (a standard commonly cited in early learning standards documents). This is, of course, an important oral language goal in long-term planning, but it is too general for guiding instructional activities over the short term. To this purpose, teachers need to focus on the particulars of a standard, that is, its indicators (sometimes referred to as examples). From the scope of the language arts standards, they need to select indicators for purposes of short-term planning in the preschool language and literacy program. Indicators provide guidance for instructional objectives that steadily steer teaching and learning activities toward the achievement of language arts standards over the program year. Consider a weekly planner for this purpose. To be effective (and practical), a weekly planner should be clear and concise, including enough details so that someone else could follow it if necessary, and short enough to fit on one piece of paper.

Look at the weekly planner example shown in Figure 2.1. It summarizes the activities in a preschool classroom during 1 week in October. Note that the planner has a place to record the current theme or unit, as well as the one that went before and the one coming up. This can help you to make connections across the many weeks of instruction. It organizes the main activities for the week, and includes relevant assessment activities. It provides space for indicating which standards areas are emphasized and encourages a coding system for recording specific performance indicators that are addressed. A space to document home–school connections is also available.

Weekly plans should reflect your long-term plan. Activities you plan each week should support children's reaching established early learning standards in oral language and early literacy knowledge and skills. They should address performance indicators that are directly linked to expected outcomes. Your weekly plans should also guide your daily planning to ensure consistency in children's language and literacy experiences. When long- and short-term plans are consistent with each other, the opportunity for children to integrate their developing language and literacy skills is greatly increased.

USING LANGUAGE AND LITERACY ASSESSMENT IN PLANNING

Assessment is an integral part of intentional teaching. It is the systematic process of collecting, reviewing, and using information from multiple sources in order to understand what children know and can do. It is the basis of informed instructional decision making, and should result in improving children's development and learning.

Two major types of assessment are used to measure young children's progress toward end-of-year expectations described in standards and outcomes. These are referred to as formative assessment and summative assessment. Both are complex assessment activities; both are central to best practice.

Last Theme: Going to School					
Current Theme/Topic: Families; Week 2					
Next Theme: My Home					

Domains: Head Start Framework	Daily Schedule				
1. Identify author and illustrator (*LKS-Book Appreciation*).				Grouping	
2. Respond orally to Big Book and read-aloud books (*LKS-Book Appreciation*).	Time	Activity	Whole Class	Small Group	Center
		Getting ready: arrival routines		X	
3. Develop family related vocabulary; Big Book new words; read-aloud new words (*LD-Receptive and Expressive Language*).		Circle I: calendar, sharing, singing	X	X	
		Shared book reading	X		
4. Communicate ideas through letter writing (*LKS-Early Writing*).		Day 1: picture walk (*My Mother Is Mine*); teach two new words	X		
5. Identify letters *M*, *m*, and /m/ sound (*LKS-Alphabet Knowledge*).		Day 2: predict/check; track print; teach two new words	X		
6. Use position words in retelling *In Between* (*LD-Expressive Language*).		Days 3–5: find words that start with *M/m*; list new words			
(Note: LKS, Literacy Knowledge & Skills; LD, Language Development)		Center/activity time		X	X
Assessment(s):		Read-alouds: *In Between Word Play*; *Time: The Color of Us*		X	X
• Friday 5-minute conference and curriculum-based measure (CBM) with children who need support.					
• Anecdotal notes on evidence of mature play in dramatic play.					
Content Standards in This Theme:		Dramatic play: family trip		X	X
• Coded identifiers from Ohio Early Learning Content standards.		Writing: family trees		X	X
(*www.ode.state.oh.us*)		Books: make a book; family scrapbook		X	X
• LL: I-5; II-4; III-6; V-4; VI-3; IIX-3; X-2		Blocks: from school to home		X	X
• M: I-1; II-3; V-1					
• SC: V-1,7					
• SS: II-1; VII-3					
Home–School: Favorite Family Story		Discovery: family graphs		X	X
		Art: family portraits		X	X
		Circle II: singing; shared writing (family letter)	X		

FIGURE 2.1. Example of a weekly planner.

In plain terms, formative assessment involves *forming judgments frequently in the flow of instruction*, whereas summative assessment focuses on *making judgments at some point in time after instruction*. Formative assessment takes place in the ebb and flow of everyday instruction. It involves systematically observing children at work and play during classroom activities, and examining children's work. Summative assessment requires that teachers stop teaching to gauge where children are at a point in time (e.g., the end of the program year). Typically a formal assessment measure is used to evaluate (judge) children's achievement in relation to a performance benchmark or one's peers.

Formative and summative assessment tools are used (1) to screen or *look at* where children are in their language development and literacy learning, (2) to progress monitor or *keep track* of where they are, and (3) to evaluate or *judge* where they are as compared with their peers or a research-based standard. Figure 2.2 illustrates the important parts of an assessment system that combine to provide a more comprehensive view of children's language and literacy learning.

In this chapter we focus on formative assessment tools for language and early literacy, since this assessment type is closest to a teacher's everyday practice. Keep in mind that formative assessment demands a knowledgeable teacher who is a careful and sensitive observer of young children.

Screening

Set aside time during the first few weeks of your program year to screen children's speaking and listening abilities, as well as their early literacy skills. The Teacher Rating of Oral Language and Literacy (TROLL; Dickinson, McCabe, & Sprague, 2003) is an informal screening measure suited to this purpose. It consists of 25 questions that assess children's language, reading, and writing on a 4-point rating scale. In the language section, for example, teachers are asked to rate a child's pattern of *asking questions* about topics that interest him or her—never, rarely, occasionally, or often. The assessment produces subscores in language use, reading, and writing, and an overall total TROLL score. This score is converted to a percentage for each child. Those children at the 50th percentile are performing at an average level. Higher percentages indicate above-average performance, and

Accountability	Screening	Instruction
◄◄◄◄◄	●●●●●	►►►►►
Looking back	*Looking at*	*Looking ahead*
Evaluate	*What is*	*What can be*
Coordinated set of multiple measures and methods		

FIGURE 2.2. The parts of an assessment system.

those at or below the 25th percentile may need further assessment and/or intervention. No formal training is required to use the TROLL measure. It requires only 5–10 minutes for each child.

Teachers can also use an observation checklist to assess children's language and literacy at different times during the program day. Different versions of such checklists can be found in professional books and journals. The speech–language therapist also can provide you with easy-to-use language observation tools. The Oral Language Checklist displayed in Figure 2.3 provides one example. Plan to focus on three to five children each day over a 2-week period to gather language use data for your entire class. You can use this information to create a language-rich environment that supports the diverse needs of young children.

Progress Monitoring

For continuous improvement in language and literacy, it is important to keep track of children's progress while they are in your program. This will allow you to determine if children's speaking, listening, reading, and writing abilities are developing adequately or need more support to thrive. Several assessment tools are available for this purpose. MyIGDIs—individual growth and development indicators—is a commercial tool that provides a comprehensive set of assessments for monitoring growth and development of young children (*www.myigdis.com*). The Literacy+ assessment set monitors skills in picture naming, rhyming, alliteration, sound identification, and visual perception.

The Oral Language Assessment Toolkit (OLAT), available through the New Teacher Center (*http://oral-language.newteachercenter.org/assessment*), is a free app that can be downloaded from iTunes. A video provides a brief overview of how to capture children's talk. Blank versions of an oral language record, record analysis, and rubric are provided. Using the oral language analysis tool, teachers can describe what they notice about a child's language use, identify strengths, consider next steps, and pinpoint how instruction might be modified to meet a child's language needs. The accompanying rubric rates language quality on a 4-point scale (e.g., *Responses are mostly simple sentences*). The app is easy to use on a regular basis, especially for monitoring the language progress of children who need more support.

Children's work samples provide yet another means of keeping track of children's progress routinely. Some products (e.g., children's writing samples), can be collected in a folder. If the children's original works cannot be saved (e.g., scribble writing a menu), a photocopy or photograph can easily be made. The same approach can be used with other products, such as three-dimensional structures the children have created and labeled. In these cases, a photograph—still or video—can be made. Because memories are short, teachers should record a brief description of the product or the activity that resulted in the product. Work samples can be assembled into a notebook or portfolio for review purposes.

Key: (+) Consistently (3) Sometimes (–) Not yet

Child Observed: _____

Observer: _____

Observational Setting

Large Group   Small Group   Individual   Comments

Date: _____

Speaking
- ☐ Responds when spoken to.
- ☐ Takes turns speaking.
- ☐ Participates in group discussions.
- ☐ Recalls and recites songs and fingerplays.
- ☐ Speaks clearly.
- ☐ Speaks in complete sentences.
- ☐ Initiates conversations.
- ☐ Asks questions.
- ☐ Tells a personal story.
- ☐ Uses appropriate sentence structure (word order, pronouns, verbs).

Listening
- ☐ Listens to rhymes, songs, and stories with interest.
- ☐ Listens to speaker in conversations.
- ☐ Follows single-step direction.
- ☐ Follows multiple-step directions.

Vocabulary
- ☐ Plays with words.
- ☐ Links new words to what is already known about a topic.
- ☐ Uses new words appropriately in conversation and discussion.

FIGURE 2.3. Oral Language Checklist. From McGraw-Hill/Wright Group (2002). Copyright 2002 by Wright Group/McGraw-Hill. Reprinted with permission of McGraw-Hill Education.

Evaluation

Assessment includes evaluation. It is necessary to find out if your program is effective and children are achieving early learning standards in language and literacy. This can be done in at least two ways. Your program may already use a commercial assessment to determine children's achievement in key areas of language and early literacy upon program completion. Examples of commercial tests include the Peabody Picture Vocabulary Test (Dunn & Dunn, 2007), the Assessment of Literacy and Language (Lombardino, Lieberman, & Brown, 2009), Get Ready to Read (Whitehurst & Lonigan, 2001), and the Woodcock–Johnson III Tests of Achievement (Woodcock, McGrew, & Mather, 2001). Check for a good match between your program goals and what the test measures before making judgments about program effectiveness. If no end-of-program assessment is required in your setting, you can repeat screening or progress monitoring tools along with your informal observations as backup, to make judgments about how well children are doing and overall program quality. Using either of these approaches, assessment results should be used to describe where children presently are in their skill development and to make improvements in your program. One of the most powerful uses of evaluation is to improve the quality of your instruction to ensure children's high achievement in essential oral language and early literacy skills related to school achievement.

SECOND-LANGUAGE DEVELOPMENT

If you have English language learners in your classroom, you should become familiar with the stages of second-language development that researchers have noted for these children. Your assessment of their progress will depend on your knowing what to expect.

Researchers have outlined the following sequence of second-language development of young children (Tabors, 2008). Of course, as with all developmental processes, there are variations in how children approach this process and how long it will take for them to go through these stages. But it is clearly important to have these stages in mind when assessing English language learners' language use in your classroom.

First, the child uses the home language. When everyone around the child is speaking a different language, there are only two options: (1) to speak the language he or she already knows, or (2) to stop speaking entirely. Many children, but not all, follow the first option for some period of time (Saville-Troike, 1987). This, of course, leads to increasing frustration, and eventually children give up trying to make others understand their language.

The second stage is the nonverbal period. After children abandon the attempt to communicate in their first language, they enter a period in which they do not talk at all. This can last for some time, or it can be a brief phase. Although they do not talk during this time, children attempt to communicate nonverbally to get help from adults or to obtain objects. Furthermore, this is a period during which children begin actively to "crack the code" of the second language. Saville-Troike (1987) noted that children will rehearse the target language by repeating what other speakers say in a low voice and by playing with the sounds of the new language.

The next stage occurs when the child is ready to go public with the new language. There are two characteristics to this speech: it is telegraphic and it involves the use of formulas. Telegraphic speech is common in early monolingual language development and involves the use of a few content words without function words or morphological markers. For example, a young child learning to speak English may say "Put paper" to convey the meaning "I want to put the paper on the table."

Formulaic speech refers to the use of unanalyzed chunks of words or routine phrases that are repetitions of what the child hears. Children use such prefabricated chunks long before they have any understanding of what they mean (Wong Fillmore, 1979).

Eventually, the child reaches the stage of productive language use. At this point the child is able to go beyond short telegraphic utterances and memorized chunks. Initially, children may form new utterances by using formulaic patterns such as "I wanna" with names for objects. In time, the child begins to demonstrate an understanding of the syntactic system of the language. Children gradually unpackage their formulas and apply newly acquired grammar rules to develop productive control over the language.

PLANNING WITH THE END IN MIND

Let's return to where we began this chapter—with early learning standards. How does the teacher plan units and daily lessons that over time reach the desired results in preschool language and literacy? Strange as it may seem, this requires thinking *backward* from the end in mind when developing each unit, topic study, or theme of instruction at any point in time.

Thinking backward involves a different kind of planning process. Instead of planning by first considering *activities* children will do, the first step is to identify *what they will learn* aligned to early learning standards. So, for example, in an upcoming study of water pipes and pumps, Ms. Campbell (a Head Start teacher) targets the following language and literacy example indicators of the Head Start Child Development and Learning Framework (2010) among other domain indicators (e.g., science):

- Comprehends increasingly complex and varied vocabulary.
- Uses increasingly complex and varied vocabulary.
- Retells stories or information from books.
- Identifies beginning and ending sounds in words.

- Recognizes words as a unit of print.
- Uses scribbles, shapes, pictures, and letters to represent objects, stories, experiences, or ideas.

The next step is to select (or develop) assessments that measure children's progress in these skill areas. At this point, most teachers need to resist the strong temptation to immediately identify instructional activities they will use and what children will do. Why? Because it is more important at this stage in planning to decide how children's learning progress will be measured to ensure they are gaining what they need to achieve end-of-year preschool language and literacy goals. In her 6-week study of water pipes and pumps, Ms. Campbell decides to use three assessments each week: (1) an oral language checklist of language interactions in different settings (whole class, play), (2) a vocabulary task that asks children to point to or name photos of terms related to the unit, and (3) a drawing/writing sample of play plans. Play plans, she reasons, will provide her with solid information about children's emerging awareness of words and the alphabetic principle. Given the busy schedule, she plans to assess only a sample of students each week—a few high-performing, typical, and lower-performing children (three to four in each group). This approach gives her a fairly accurate picture of how the whole class is doing.

The final step is to choose and sequence the key instructional activities each week that will engage children and exercise their speaking, listening, reading, and writing skills. This is a most enjoyable stage of planning because teachers can use their creativity and imagination to select and develop learning activities that are engaging and challenging. Here are a few of the learning activities that occurred in Ms. Campbell's classroom:

- Observing the flow of water in gutters, hoses, and pipes to understand factors that affect water flow.
- Mapping the locations and routes of pipes in the school and at home; talking with the custodian about the functions of pipes in various areas of the school building.
- Measuring pipes.
- Making three-dimensional models of water systems.
- Weighing containers of water.
- Creating and reading charts.
- Learning about jobs at the water department.

IMPLEMENTING PLANNING IN THE CLASSROOM

In a song to his son Sean, John Lennon sang the line "Life is what happens to you while you're busy making other plans." So it often seems. As every teacher knows, the best-laid plans can go awry because classroom life is unpredictable.

The unexpected happens (unexpectedly). Instructional plans, however, can unfold effectively most of the time when structures are put into place that support the routines, regularities, and rules of classroom life.

Routines

The first order of routine involves organizing the day into blocks of time for purposeful activity. The typical preschool day includes the following blocks of time that are filled with opportunities for speaking, listening, reading, and writing:

Greeting Time

In addition to modeling and exchanging social courtesies that encourage speaking and listening, greeting time is an ideal opportunity for children to link language and literacy. One good idea is to have children "sign in" by writing their first names (or making their mark) on chart paper at an easel. See Figure 2.4 for a sign-in procedure that requires children to write their first names as a daily attendance activity. Children's names are their first "decoders," helping them to learn alphabet letter names and sounds.

Activity Time

Much of activity time (play and table work) should be filled with language as children play together and work on small projects with adults. These are opportune times for conversation, discussion, and role play. You should also deliberately use these times for modeling how to ask questions to clarify or gain information or analyze and explore ideas, and to prompt children to find solutions to questions such as "Why do our shadows become longer or shorter?" or "What does the architect do?" For English language learners you may want to model how children can ask for help from others (e.g., "Say to Sammy, 'May I have some play dough?' ").

---

1. Prepare a sign-in sheet with the names of four or five children on each page.

2. Tell the children, "I need your help to keep daily attendance. Every day when you arrive, you will sign in. You will put your name on this sign-in sheet. Here's what you do. Find your name on the sign-in sheet. Write your name in the box next to it as best as you can. This is your signature. When you sign in, we all know you are here with us today."

3. Show the children how to follow the steps: arrive, go to the sign-in spot, find your name on the sheet, sign in.

4. Maintain the sign-in sheets in a folder to note children's progress in name writing.

FIGURE 2.4. Example of a sign-in procedure. Based on McGee and Richgels (2003).

Circle Time

Beyond shared reading and sharing time, consider using circle time for developing children's storytelling abilities and listening comprehension. Tell stories to children drawn from your own childhood memories. Assist children in having ideas about stories they can tell. Help them prepare. Invite them to share their own stories with the group. A storytelling program gives children practice in speaking in front of an audience, develops their sense of story, exercises their use of decontextualized speech, and is personally meaningful for them. These activities may be particularly challenging for English language learners. Make sure that they are ready to participate actively in these events. If they are not ready, find another activity that they can be part of that will let them show off their growing language competence.

Outdoor Time

Use outdoor time for extending language and literacy experiences by modeling new games children can play and for assisting children in using language effectively to negotiate the rules and procedures for play and to resolve conflicts. On neighborhood outings with the children, point out environmental print that is present on stores and businesses, posters and storefront advertisements, traffic signs, and so on. Carry information gathered on these walks back to your settings, incorporating it into your instruction and play areas.

Regularities

Instructional time well spent involves teachers interacting with the whole class and small groups, and helping children play well with one another. When working with the whole class teachers should include some direct teaching and demonstrating of effective speaking and listening skills. For example, a teacher might role-play language and appropriate behavior for buying or selling in the class Grocery Store. Plan to spend about 10–15 minutes each day teaching specific concepts and skills for talking, reading, and writing with a whole class of preschoolers. Teachers should group children in pairs or small groups (three or four children) for instructional purposes. Children make better progress in these situations because they have more chances to use and attend to language under the guidance of an adult.

There are two different types of groups that work well: heterogeneous groups and homogeneous groups. Heterogeneous groups are made up of children with different ability levels; homogeneous groups gather together children with similar strengths and weaknesses. Neither type of group should be seen as permanent but rather as flexible, with children leaving and joining different groups depending on the instructional purpose. For example, you might gather one or two small heterogeneous groups together to make a sand clock in the whole-class exploration of time and timekeepers. Later, homogeneous groups of children may be formed for board games and puzzles that develop alphabet letter knowledge. This allows you to pitch your instruction so that it is neither too hard nor too easy for any one child in the group. If you have English language learners in your classroom, consider how you can alternate their experiences, sometimes having them work with children who are more fluent in English and sometimes having them work in groups with other English language learners, so that you can tailor instruction to their needs.

One major concern for preschool teachers is ensuring all children are actively engaged during small-group time. Inviting, yet challenging play activity is key! Create play areas that stimulate pretending, enrich content knowledge, and involve complex roles or processes. In the water pipes and pumps unit, for example, Ms. Campbell (with the children's help) created the Plumbing Shop, complete with plastic pipe of different diameters, plastic tubing, PVC pipe and connectors, T and Y joints (elbow joints were a favorite), nozzles, faucet handles (C for cold; H for hot), shower heads, pipe wrenches, small pails, pumps, and, of course, expert plumbers. The "plumbers" even prepared a display of how pipes work and placed it outside the classroom door (see Figure 2.5). Parents were impressed!

In the classroom, focus on creating five well-designed play areas: (1) art with ample supplies for creating products, (2) library corner with plenty of print books and e-books for listening and browsing (note: it should be comfy), (3) blocks of all sizes for large- and small-scale constructions, (4) discovery for experimenting and problem solving, and (5) dramatic play for stretching the imagination. Set up your small-group time to support independent play activity, as well as to provide more structured instruction in a playful context. Allow sufficient time for uninterrupted play, at least 45–60 minutes daily (Johnson, Christie, & Wardle, 2005). Help children make a plan for their play, periodically checking in on their

FIGURE 2.5. Plumbing display in the classroom.

progress, and coaching them on the spot when they need help. Satisfying, rich play influences children's thought and language substantially (Smith, 2007). It allows children to think and do with language and literacy at a higher level than when in a real situation. It helps them to manipulate abstract ideas and thinking skills that further oral language comprehension. Because play requires children to conform to roles and rules, it helps them practice self-regulation in thinking and actions (Diamond, Barnett, Thomas, & Munro, 2007). For these reasons, play needs to be an integral part of small-group activities. It provides powerful growth-producing experiences for young children. Table 2.1 describes the characteristics of mature play that should be present by the end of kindergarten.

Rules

For any place to run smoothly, it is necessary to establish rules that outline appropriate ways of interacting with others and standards of acceptable work. Children need to know what is expected of them. It is a good idea to post a daily schedule that shows the flow of the day. The schedule helps everyone to remember what comes next and also provides a written record of what has been accomplished. Discussion of the daily schedule can become part of the everyday routine and at the same time draw children's attention to print and its uses. English language learners will find this routine extremely useful, as it will make the daily flow of activities predictable, enabling them to show that they know what is going on in the classroom.

Another useful tool is a play-area board for organizing and managing children's play time. Different colors can be used to represent different core play areas—for example, green for library (reading and writing), purple for discovery, orange for blocks, red for art, blue for dramatic play. Children make their choices and take a colored clip or a similar reminder (e.g., a badge or necklace) to the play area. Play areas should be limited to four or five children at one time.

TABLE 2.1. Characteristics of Mature Play

Characteristic	Example
Symbolic representations and symbolic actions	"Would you come with us? Let's go to Sea World."
Complex interwoven themes	"We're following the treasure map to the scary mountain."
Complex interwoven roles	"You can be the customers and I'm the cash register guy. Jared's the waiter guy. OK?"
Extended time frame (over several days)	After 2 days: "We're still playing hospital and the babies got so-o-o sick."

You will need to teach the children how to use the play board, which will require several weeks of practice. But this is time well spent because it reduces interruptions while you are with small groups, and it encourages children to take charge of their own play activity. Use of the board also benefits children's print awareness because they quickly learn to recognize their own as well as their class-mates' names as play areas are selected. Some soon learn to read the names for the different play areas.

For children to work independently at an activity they need to know the rules that apply and the consequences of not abiding by the rules. You should ask the children to help you make the rules for work and play. One way to begin is to ask the children why it is necessary to have rules. Make a list of their responses on chart paper. Ask them what would be good rules for playtime activities; list these as well. Children usually come up with negative statements, such as "No hitting." When all the children have had a chance to contribute, ask them to help you group like rules into categories—for example: No hitting, No punching, Don't throw books, Don't spit on books, Don't leave things out, and Don't yell at each other. Ask the children to help you make a label for each group and guide them toward positive statements such as "Treat others kindly," "Work together," "Make room for others," "Put things away," "Use materials carefully," and "Use quiet voices."

Post the rules where children can easily see them, and refer to them when introducing new activities. If you consistently refer to the rules from the begin-ning of the year, children will soon learn what is expected of them in work and play activities. If you find that there are English language learners who are having difficulty with the rules, it may be that there is miscommunication about what is expected. Working directly with parents on these issues and asking parents to explain the rules to their children may help the situation.

MAKING THE MOST OF RESOURCES

Every early childhood setting contains resources in terms of time, people, and materials. Your careful use of these resources can maximize children's language and literacy experiences to the fullest. You need to set up your daily schedule with an emphasis on children's active learning with you and their peers in uninter-rupted time blocks. Snack time, for example, is an informal time for talking, just as naptime is a stretch of time for listening to stories and pretending to read all by oneself.

Adults are one of the richest resources for children because they can bring considerable knowledge, language, and print to them. One effective way to involve adults is to have them participate in topics or themes you are exploring with the children. For example, when Ben Mardell's preschoolers studied squirrels, he invited Judy Chupasko from the Mammalian Department at Harvard University's

Museum of Comparative Zoology to his class (see Mardell, 1999). Judy explained the preparation of animals used in scientific study, which fascinated the children and also introduced them to the idea of anatomy—mapping the insides of things.

Teacher assistants are an excellent resource in supporting the language and literacy curriculum. They can assist with progress monitoring and other assessment activities. They should be actively involved in your read-aloud program, reading at least two or three books per day to small groups of children or individual children. And they should be richly supporting children's project activities and dramatic play. Working as a team, you and your teaching assistant greatly increase the learning potential of the preschool environment.

Involve parent volunteers meaningfully in the day-to-day. They can join children at play on a regular basis. In this informal setting they can watch and learn, they can take roles and participate, or they can show children how to play a game. Adult presence is encouraging to children and stimulates them to play for longer periods of time. When adults join in they engage children in conversation; they use new words and more complex sentences that enrich children's speaking and listening (Neuman & Roskos, 2007).

For second-language learners, make time to bring their home languages into your classroom. Often, teaching assistants are fluent in a language other than English and can read a familiar book to the whole class in that language. Or parents can come into the class to read in their home language. The children whose home language is being used will be thrilled, and the other children will get to hear the sounds and vocabulary of another language.

Materials are the stock-in-trade of a well-provisioned early learning environment. Along with everyday supplies such as writing tools, equipment, and charts, they include the books, toys, software, e-books, apps, digital tools (e.g., iPads), and websites that widen the world of preschoolers. Materials should be of high quality to engage preschoolers' active minds as well as their active bodies. And they should represent the cultural diversity of the children in the classroom. The Early Literacy Materials Selector (ELMS) is a tool that can be used to review early literacy materials for purchase or those already being used in a program (Roskos, Lenhart, & Noll, 2012). The tool is designed to assist early childhood educators and administrators in evaluating the quality and instructional guidance provided by early literacy curriculum materials and commercial programs. It offers a systematic approach to the review of early literacy curriculum materials based on evidence-based criteria of product quality.

CONCLUSION

To close this chapter, here are a few memorable ideas. Early childhood settings where children talk, read, and write a lot are the result of thoughtful planning. Long-term planning involves goal setting using state-level early learning standards and/or the Head Start Child and Learning Development Framework (2010). Early childhood teachers should also be alert to the CCSS-ELA for kindergarten, and set children on a good pace to achieving these goals. A weekly planner works well for short-term planning where the teacher identifies weekly ELA objectives. Formative and summative assessments inform instructional planning. Teachers should plan for systematic formative assessment in their instruction. Various classroom-based assessments can be used for screening, progress monitoring, and evaluating children's development and growth in the language arts. Teachers should take second-language development into account when planning weekly lessons and assessment activities. Planning with the end in mind helps teachers to keep learning outcomes in mind while planning units, as well as for the day-to-day. Routines, regularities, and rules can support the implementation of plans, although teachers need to remain flexible and responsive to the unexpected. Finally, teachers need to make the most of the resources they have (time, people, materials) to create a high-quality language and literacy environment for all the young children in the program.

Preschool in Practice

Implementing Play Planning

Older preschoolers can be guided to plan for play to their advantage. Play planning helps to facilitate the development of mature play skills—such as imagination, role taking, negotiation, and persistence—that in turn foster other developmental areas, such as content knowledge, problem solving, and language (Bodrova & Leong, 2007). Play planning also has been found to support the development of self-regulation skills (Diamond et al., 2007).

Successful implementation of play planning in the classroom requires considerable instructional planning on the part of the teacher. The key planning steps are outlined below. (For a more detailed description of how to implement play planning, see Roskos & Christie, 2013.)

Getting Started

Establish primary play areas (e.g., art, blocks, discovery, dramatic play, library/literacy) in the classroom and color code them (e.g., red, blue, green, yellow, brown) both in terms of signage and management for play activity.

Weeks 1–2: Choose–Say–Go

Explain to the children that they will start to "plan" for their play. Model how to choose a place to play, say its name, and then go to the area to play. Show each play area and rehearse the planning approach. Then start the choose–say–go routine. Each child chooses and then says where he or she will go (names it) and provides a bit of information about what he or she plans to do there.

Weeks 3–4 (or Longer): Choose–Say–Draw–Go

Once children are familiar with the choose–say–go routine, introduce the idea of a play plan "picture." Model how to make a play plan by (1) writing your name, (2) drawing where you want to play, (3) making a line, and (4) putting the name of the play area on the line. Tell children they will choose–say–then draw what they plan to do. Assist those children who appear ready for this step; others can continue to choose–say–go. Once children start to play, encourage them to stick with their plan to the extent possible.

Weeks 5–6 (or Longer): Choose–Say–Draw–Write–Go

Continue with the draw portion until you have a well-established routine. Collect the children's play plans every day and use them to monitor individual student progress. When you observe that about 60% of the older children can choose–say–draw–go, then introduce the next level—how to write a play plan. Model how to (1) write your name, (2) say what you plan to play, (3) draw a picture, (4) make a line for each word in your plan and attempt to write the word on the line (e.g., <u>I will</u> <u>be</u> <u>a</u> <u>cook</u>). Assist those children who appear ready to try. Tell the children that making play plans takes practice—and to do their best.

Weeks 6 and Beyond

Continue to model and scaffold the play planning process, including more and more older children in drawing and writing their play plans. Display play plans, and also assemble them into play plan books that children can review and share.

Choosing Quality Early Literacy Materials

The explosion of early literacy materials for young children is a real boon to busy early childhood teachers. But this *blessing of riches* also comes with a responsibility to make the best choices about which materials to select and use with young children. Materials are the instructional resources that support instruction in an educational setting. They are the *durable goods* of teaching, so to speak. While materials alone do not teach children, they certainly do affect our teaching. Materials matter!

The early childhood teachers in the Hudson School District are in the process of selecting a PreK–K early literacy program. They agree that the early literacy program for 4-year-olds should build foundations for kindergarten literacy instruction. They decide to use the ELMS to guide their evaluation of available programs (Roskos et al., 2012). The tool is organized into four parts.

Part I consists of a materials inventory that identifies the primary items and how many are available for instruction. Taking an inventory of an early literacy program is often overlooked, but it is very important. It helps teachers to organize and list curricular materials by type and amount, sort of like filling the shopping cart when online shopping.

Part II provides criteria for rating the quality of materials contained within the program in key categories of instructional stuff (resources). Part II of the tool assesses the design quality of the program materials. Three criteria are used to describe design quality: availability of materials; sufficient amount of them; and usability in terms of organization, appropriateness, and appeal. Some programs, for example, offer too few materials for adequate instruction while others may be too hard to implement.

Part III describes a method for systematically examining the directions given for instruction in essential early literacy skills: oral language, vocabulary, phonological awareness, alphabet letter knowledge, print knowledge, writing, and differentiating instruction.

Part IV provides an overall product review of the curriculum or program as a set of materials for early literacy instruction. It provides a rating (score) that describes general patterns of instruction (e.g., letters and sounds, print concepts, or language comprehension).

Using a team approach, the early childhood teachers set aside time on a districtwide professional day to review their top program choices. After familiarizing themselves with the evaluation tool, they worked in pairs to conduct a review of each early literacy program. Each pair inventoried the program contents, rated the quality of materials, and analyzed the directions for evidence-based practices. At the end of the review process, pairs determined their final scores for each program. Each pair also shared any final or conclusive questions, comments, and concerns about each program reviewed, including the quantity and quality of the product materials and the directions provided in the teacher manuals. Summative discussions centered on the strengths and weaknesses of each program. This discussion then led to rank ordering the programs from strongest to weakest and making a final decision for program selection.

IDEAS FOR DISCUSSION, REFLECTION, AND ACTION

1. Arrange to interview two preschool teachers, each in a different early childhood setting. Ask and record answers to the following questions:

   - "What resources/materials do you use to plan your daily lessons?"
   - "Is there a standard lesson plan form? If so, what does it look like?"
   - "How is your lesson plan shared with others (e.g., teachers, supervisors, parents)?"
   - "How is ongoing assessment included in the daily lesson plan?"
   - "How do teachers collaborate on unit plans and lesson plans?"

   Organize and share your interview data with a peer who has also conducted interviews. What patterns do you notice in the planning process?

2. Using the Oral Language Checklist in Figure 2.3, evaluate a child's oral language in your class. If you are not yet teaching, arrange to spend some time with a preschool child. Fill in the checklist based on a recorded and transcribed discussion that you had with the child. Evaluate the observational checklist and determine in what areas the child needs to improve. Provide a list of activities that could be helpful in promoting the child's language development.

3. We live in a country that is very diverse. Many of the children who enter preschool speak another language than English. Ideas for accommodating the needs of English language learners are mentioned throughout this chapter. Compile a list of these ideas and add new ones of your own that will help these children learn English while maintaining their first languages.

CHAPTER 3

Literacy Centers and Activities

Looking into Ms. Lynch's classroom of 4-year-olds, it is clear that the children are actively engaged in several different literacy center activities. Louis and Ramon are squeezed tightly into a rocking chair, sharing a book. Marcel, Patrick, and Roseangela snuggle under a shelf—a private spot filled with stuffed animals. They take turns with their pretend reading. Tesha and Tiffany are on the floor with a felt-board and character cutouts from *The Gingerbread Boy* (Galdone, 1983), alternately telling the story and manipulating the figures: "Run, run as fast as you can! You

can't catch me, I'm the Gingerbread Man!" Four children listen to tapes of *Pierre* (Sendak, 1991) on headsets, each child holding a copy of the book and chanting along with the narrator, "I don't care, I don't care."

Children in classrooms with classroom literacy centers read and look at books much more often than children in classrooms without such collections. The efforts spent in creating an inviting atmosphere for a classroom literacy center are rewarded by increased interest in books (Guthrie, 2002; Gambrell, 2009; Wooten & Cullinan, 2009).

PHYSICAL SPACE IN THE LITERACY CENTER

The physical features of a classroom literacy center can play an important role in motivating children to use that area. Well-designed classroom literacy centers significantly increase the number of children who choose to participate in literature activities during free-choice periods. Conversely, in classrooms where the classroom literacy center is poorly designed, literature activities are among the least popular choices during free-choice periods (Morrow, 2002, 2015).

The classroom literacy center should be a focal area in a preschool classroom, immediately visible and inviting to anyone entering the room. However, many children crave privacy; sometimes they will look at a book in a coat closet or under a shelf. To provide some solitude, the center can be partitioned on two sides with bookshelves, a piano, file cabinets, or freestanding bulletin boards. Children can listen to recorded books with headsets to get a break from the commotion of the classroom. Alternatively, children can use a painted appliance carton as a cozy reading nook. The dimensions of the literacy center will vary with the size of the classroom. Generally, it should be large enough to accommodate five or six children comfortably. Figure 3.1 illustrates the design of an effective preschool literacy center.

In a digital age, the physical environment should also support young children's interactions with digital books and apps. Relatively little is known about the impact of e-book devices, such as touch screen computers, interactive white boards, and mobile devices, on the arrangement and allocation of classroom space. The architectural goal is to weave e-book browsing and reading into already well-designed physical learning spaces of the classroom, and not to isolate this way of reading from traditional book reading areas in the literacy center (Lackney, 2003). Appealing spaces for e-book browsing and reading, and app exploration on digital tools, include (1) clearly defined space in the book or library corner; (2) signage related to e-book titles, usage and storage; (3) inviting cafélike surroundings for sharing e-books with friends or enjoying them in private; (4) good acoustics to hear stories; and (5) access to headphones, adequate Wi-Fi, and power outlets for devices and recharging stations. Inviting e-book nooks are popular places that

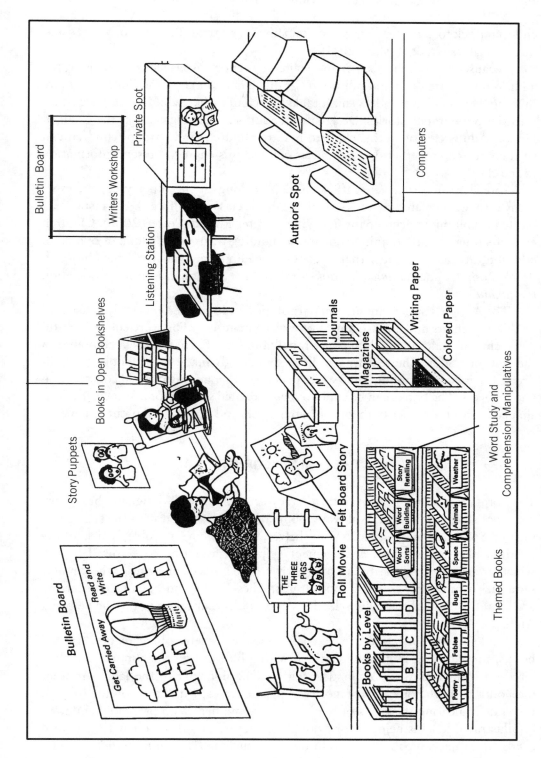

FIGURE 3.1. A classroom literacy center.

children flock to at center time and enjoy, supporting their literacy motivations and interests (Burstein & Roskos, 2011).

Because much of the activity in the literacy center takes place on the floor, the addition of an area rug and pillows or beanbag chairs makes the floor area more inviting. If possible, include a small table and chairs where children can use headsets to listen to taped stories. Designate an adult-size rocking chair as the Chair of Honor. Adults can sit in this chair to read to children, and pairs of children can sit there to read together. Invited guests can use this chair to present information to the class.

Soft elements, such as stuffed animals, belong in the literacy center, especially if they are related to books available in the classroom library. For instance, a stuffed rabbit might accompany *The Tale of Peter Rabbit* (Potter, 2006). Children enjoy reading to stuffed animals or simply holding them as they look at books. In addition, attractive posters that encourage reading are available from the Children's Book Council (*www.cbcbooks.org*) and the American Library Association (*www.ala.org*).

The Author's Spot is an integral part of the literacy center. It usually consists of a table and chairs and an assortment of writing materials. There are colored felt-tip pens, crayons, and lined white paper ranging in size. There may be a computer in the Author's Spot. The teacher can have some ready-made blank books for children to write in by stapling some white paper together adding colored construction paper covers. The books can be cut into theme-related shapes; for instance, use fish-shaped books for an ocean theme or butterfly-shaped books for a nature theme.

THE LIBRARY CORNER

The library corner is one part of the literacy center. In a well-designed library corner, books are stored in several ways. Some books are shelved with the spines facing out. Some are on open-faced bookshelves, with the covers visible, which allows children easy access. This arrangement helps call attention to featured books, which are changed regularly. An alternative to open-faced shelving is the circular wire rack, commonly found in bookstores. These racks and open-faced shelving are ideal for highlighting new selections and books that relate to the theme being studied.

Books in the collection can be color coded and shelved by category. Animal books, for example, might be identified with a blue dot on their spines and clustered on a shelf marked "Animals," with a blue dot next to the label. Another method is to store books by categories in plastic crates, with labels on the front of the crate indicating the types of books in the container. With preschool children, an illustrated label is helpful; for example, a picture of a dinosaur with the word *dinosaur* can accompany books on this topic, such as *Dinosaur Thunder* (Bauer, 2012) and *How Do Dinosaurs Play with Their Friends?* (Yolen, 2006).

How big should the classroom library collection be? A preschool classroom library should offer five to eight books per child, with books ranging across three to four levels of difficulty. It is advisable to stock multiple copies of some books. Children enjoy looking at the same book with a friend (Morrow, 1985). The collection should include narrative fiction and informational nonfiction (sometimes referred to as expository text). In the past, collections for early childhood were almost exclusively narrative stories. However, as adults, most of the material we read is nonfiction; for this reason, children need a lot of experience with informational text. Now educators have come to realize that informational, nonfiction books should comprise one-third to one-half of the total selections in a preschool classroom library (Duke, 2004; Moss, Leone, & Dipillo, 1997).

Books and other reading materials are easy to accumulate. They can be purchased inexpensively at yard sales or flea markets. Teachers can borrow up to 20 books a month from most public libraries, ask for book donations from parents, and hold fund raisers for book purchases. In addition, children's paperback book clubs offer inexpensive books and free bonus books with bulk purchases. Children's magazines and newspapers belong in the classroom library, too, even if they are not current. For the cost of mailing and shipping, some publishers and local magazine agencies will donate outdated periodicals to schools. To ensure continued interest, the teacher can introduce new books and materials in the library corner. We suggest introducing about 20 new books each month, replacing 20 that have been there for a while. The 20 new books can be selections that have been stored in the closet for a while. By continuing this rotation, "old" books will be greeted as new friends a few months later. Circulating books can also help compensate for a limited budget. The evaluation checklist in Figure 3.2 can help you decide if books and other resources are appropriate for your classroom library.

Establish a classroom system for children to check out the books. Preschool children need adult assistance to check out and return books. The checkout system should be simple, such as copying titles and recording dates on index cards filed under the child's name. Another method for checking out books is to use a loose-leaf notebook with a page for each child to record books taken out and returned.

Types of Books in the Library Corner

Books and other materials selected for the library corner should appeal to a variety of interests and span a range of levels. Preschoolers enjoy reading cloth books and board books, as well as hardback and paperback books.

Picture Storybooks

When we think of children's literature, most often we think of picture storybooks, in which the text is closely associated with the illustrations. A good picture storybook will include a setting, theme, plot, and resolution. Picture storybooks are

Books
Is the book age appropriate?

_____ The children can relate the story to their lives and past experiences.

_____ The children can identify with characters.

_____ There is directly quoted conversation.

_____ The children will benefit from the attitudes and models in the story.

Does the book teach early literacy?

_____ The book can be used to expand knowledge.

_____ There is new, related vocabulary.

_____ The book increases or broadens understanding.

_____ The book is clearly written with a vocabulary and sequence that the children can understand.

_____ Repetitions of words, actions, rhymes, or story parts are used.

_____ The story structure is evident with a beginning, middle, and end.

_____ The story includes humorous events and silly names.

What are some key criteria in choosing books?

_____ The text is not too long to sit through.

_____ There are not too many words to read.

_____ There are enough colorful or action-packed pictures or illustrations to hold the children's attention.

_____ The children can participate in the story by speaking or making actions.

_____ The story is not too complex, symbolic, or confusing for the children.

Toys
Is the toy age appropriate?

_____ The toy is the correct age level for the children.

_____ Special instructions are not necessary to play with the toy.

_____ Children cannot harm themselves unintentionally with the toy.

(continued)

FIGURE 3.2. Evaluation checklist for books, toys, websites, and software.

Does the toy teach early literacy?

_____ The toy can be used in relation to storytelling.

_____ The toy provides opportunities to expand vocabulary.

_____ The toy has writing on it that correlates with actions being done.

_____ There are opportunities for children to practice new vocabulary using the toy.

_____ The toy increases or broadens understanding.

What are some key criteria in choosing toys?

_____ The children are interested in the toy.

_____ The toy is reusable.

_____ The toy can be integrated into current or future lessons.

_____ The toy is durable.

_____ There are materials included with the toy for parents/teacher to use with the toy.

Websites and Software

Is the website or software age appropriate?

_____ The children can understand the directions to use the website or software.

_____ The instructions are easy to follow or relay to the children.

_____ The website or software provides separate instructions for the parent or teacher.

Does the website or software teach early literacy?

_____ The website or software can be used by the parent or teacher in a special way.

_____ The website or software offers new vocabulary.

_____ The website or software increases or broadens understanding.

_____ The website or software is written clearly with a vocabulary and sequence that children can understand.

_____ There are repetitions of words, actions, or rhymes.

_____ The website or software has humorous parts and silly names.

What are some key criteria in choosing a proper website or software?

_____ The parent or teacher enjoys using the website or software.

_____ There are no confusing parts that the teacher or parent does not understand.

_____ The children are able to follow the instructions with a parent or teacher present.

_____ The website or software is challenging and provides opportunities for increasing skills.

FIGURE 3.2. *(continued)*

available on a wide range of topics, and many are known for their excellence. The Caldecott Medal is awarded annually to the illustrator of an outstanding picture storybook; any classroom library should include an assortment of Caldecott-winning books. For example, a very popular book with children is *Where the Wild Things Are* by Maurice Sendak, which was a Caldecott Medal winner in 1963.

Realistic literature is a subcategory of picture storybooks that deals with real-life issues. For preschool children, two common problems are bedtime fears and coping when a new baby joins the family. Other topics of interest might include visits to the doctor and the dentist.

Picture Concept Books

Picture concept books are appropriate for the very young child. Most picture concept books do not have story lines, though they often have themes, such as animals or food. Each page usually includes a picture identified by a printed word. Many picture concept books are made of cardboard, cloth, or vinyl to withstand rigorous handling. Alphabet and number books are also considered picture concept books.

Traditional Literature

Traditional literature includes nursery rhymes, folktales, fairytales, and other familiar stories that are part of our heritage and originated in the oral tradition of storytelling. We often assume that children are familiar with *Goldilocks and the Three Bears* (Brett, 1992) and *The Three Little Pigs* (Galdone, 1984), yet many children have not been exposed to these traditional stories. Children who do know the stories welcome them as old friends. Folktales are often retold in picture-book style. Many of these stories originate in other countries and cultures, and therefore broaden a child's experience and knowledge base.

Poetry

Poetry is too often forgotten in collections of children's literature. Many themed anthologies have been compiled for young children, and they should be an important part of the library corner.

Big Books

Big Books, oversized picture books that rest on an easel, allow groups of children to see the pictures and the print as it is being read. They may be either enlarged versions of books originally published in a different format, or books written specifically for the Big Book format. Big Books help young children to make the association between oral and written language and make it easy for teachers to demonstrate how print is read from left to right across the page.

Predictable Books

Predictable literature features rhyme; repetition; catchphrases; familiar sequences, such as days of the week or numbers; cumulative patterns, in which events are repeated or added on as the story continues; stories about familiar topics; and familiar or popular stories. Predictability could appear in any type of genre. Children particularly benefit from predictable literature. Predictability helps children understand the story line more easily and enables them to join in as the book is read aloud.

Informational Books

As mentioned early in this chapter, informational books are nonfiction books. These books broaden children's background information, help them to explore new ideas, and often stimulate a deep interest in a particular topic. Quality informational text will follow a definitive structure such as description, sequence, compare and contrast, cause and effect, or problem and solution. Preschoolers generally enjoy books about topics such as communities, dinosaurs, and famous people. Informational texts for preschoolers also can include menus, signs, newspapers, greeting cards, recipes, and so on.

Surveys of early childhood classrooms show that informational text comprises a very small proportion—less than 15%—of the materials read aloud (Yopp & Yopp, 2000). The common belief has been that children should learn to read and listen to narrative text in the early childhood years and then progress to reading informational text to learn information in the elementary grades. However, this approach can cause difficulty for students when they enter fourth grade and are suddenly expected to read informational text but have little experience with the genre. It simply isn't true that 3- to 8-year-olds are too young to understand and enjoy informational books. When selecting books to read for your classroom, be sure to choose both informational and narrative text. See Appendix A for lists of quality children's literature of many types.

New Literacies and E-Books?

The term *new literacies* refers to multiple literacies in a world of multimodal communications from e-mails to reports to books, to assessments and to websites. New literacies use new, digital, and multimedia tools to access information (e.g., electronic tablets) and express identity (e.g., Facebook). Our young children are growing up in a world of new literacies where e-books, apps, and interactive games are rapidly joining traditional storybooks as sources of print interactions. Web-based media provide a rich store of new literacies. For example, you can (1) find online books to read to children, (2) use the Internet for searching out information, (3) e-mail messages to correspond with others, and (4) create websites (e.g., Moodle) to post children's work (e.g., responses to literature).

In the growing store of new literacies materials, e-books are spreading rapidly into early childhood classrooms, inviting children to interact with books in multimodal ways. E-books offer rich, multisensory reading experiences for young children beyond the age of 2. Adults and teachers can and should support e-book shared reading providing a warm, enjoyable, and educative experience. Several sources of quality e-books are listed below.

Digital Storytime

Digital Storytime (*http://digital-storytime.com*) is a blog founded by Carisa Kluver, a mom and educator, and her husband Marc, who is an app developer. Carisa reviews children's interactive e-books and her detailed ratings and information are posted on the site. You can search the reviews by several categories, including age range, price range, or quality. Carisa also runs a corresponding Twitter account where she'll occasionally share updates and notify followers about free apps or special deals.

Children's Technology Review

Children's Technology Review (*http://childrenstech.com*) is an online source edited by Warren Buckleitner. For a small subscription fee ($8/month), the site provides complete and objective reviews of a full range of interactive media products for children. A newsletter (.pdf) is published monthly plus every Wednesday morning a weekly newsletter is sent that features three noteworthy children's apps. The most recent included Bugs and Buttons 2 (math and logic activities for children ages 3–12), Disney Animated (all ages), and Quick-Tap Spanish (ages 5–11). All products are kid tested and archived at Mediatech Foundation. The Children's Technology Review site is a treasure trove of information for educators and parents!

Little eLit

Little eLit (*http://littleelit.com*) is another excellent resource for parents and teachers of preschoolers. Produced by Cen Campbell, a children's librarian, Little eLit reviews apps and e-books for children ages 2–5; it also maintains a current list of other review resources that provide information about digital and media literacy for young children. The monthly archives on the site are a storehouse of information about how to share apps and e-books with young children.

Your Local Library

Your local library is a great resource for learning more about e-books. Increasingly, children's librarians are *media mentors* who can lead the way in the intentional and appropriate use of dynamic technologies with our new emergent readers. They can point adults in the direction of reviews of e-book apps for children. *Kirkus Reviews*, for example, provides a list of the Best Book Apps for toddlers to teens (*www.kirkusreviews.com/book-reviews/ipad*). See Appendix B for more information on e-books for children.

The Importance of Quality

Whatever materials you select for your classroom, it is important to pay attention to quality. Good picture books include clear and uncluttered illustrations. Quality narrative texts feature the following characteristics:

- A vivid setting and well-delineated characters.
- A well-designed theme concerning the problem or goal of the main character.
- A series of episodes or plot points that help the main character to solve his or her problem or achieve the goal.
- A resolution in which the problem is solved or the goal is achieved.

Quality informational texts feature one or more of the following structures (Vukelich, Evans, & Albertson, 2003):

- *Description*: Gives the reader a picture of the subject based on story observation.
- *Sequence*: Explains the steps that produce a certain product or outcome.
- *Comparison and contrast*: Comparisons are usually made in two ways. In block comparisons, two items with a similar classification are compared and then contrasted. In point-by-point comparisons, similarities and differences are compared alternately.
- *Cause and effect*: Causality tells why something happens.
- *Problem and solution*: A problem is presented, followed by its solution. An understanding of chronology is necessary to comprehend this structure.
- *Exemplification (reason and example)*: The main idea is printed with supporting details.

STORYBOOK READING PRACTICES IN THE LITERACY CENTER

The most important thing we can do to promote literacy development is to read to children. Being read to helps children develop positive attitudes toward reading. The ritual of reading promotes sharing and the warm feelings that are generated by a storybook reading remain long after the story ends. Some stories take on a special meaning as they become favorites between an adult and a child.

The storybook reading experience must be pleasant and interactive to be beneficial. It is important to establish a relaxed atmosphere and to designate a special location for read-alouds. A rocking chair in the literacy center is a perfect spot for sharing books. You may wish to let children take turns sitting near you in the rocking chair during story time, with the other children in a single or double semicircle. Because children enjoy seeing illustrations during story reading, hold the book so that it faces the group or pause periodically and turn the book so its pictures can be seen.

A story reading is like a dramatic presentation. Before reading a story to children, practice reading it aloud to yourself. Be expressive when you read a book to children. Match your voice and facial expressions to the character who is speaking. Read slowly and with a great deal of animation. Record or videotape your readings so you can evaluate and improve your technique. Begin each story with an introduction and set a purpose for reading to enhance comprehension, as shown in this example:

> "Today I'm going to read a book about a little boy who has a new baby in the house. Now he has to share his things, which he never had to do before. The name of the book is *Peter's Chair*. The author is Ezra Jack Keats [1998]. While I read the story, think about the part of the story you like best. If you have a younger brother or sister, think about some of the ways in which your family is similar to Peter's."

When you have finished reading the book, begin a discussion with questions such as "What part of the story did you like best?"; "Who has a brother or sister?"; "Have you ever had any problems with your brother, sister, or a friend? What happened? How did you solve the problem?" These questions reflect the purpose stated at the beginning of the reading and enhance comprehension.

Interest heightens when stories are discussed both before and after reading, especially if they are related to issues that reflect children's real-life experiences or current school topics. Storybook reading activities offer an ideal opportunity to help children develop comprehension skills. This is illustrated in the following interactive story discussion, in which Ms. Elizabeth, a preschool teacher, leads a discussion with 4-year-olds after reading *Peter and the Wolf* (Prokofiev, 1986).

MS. ELIZABETH: Which characters were good and which were bad?

JAZMIN: The wolf was bad, but everyone else was good.

MS. ELIZABETH: Why do you think that?

JAZMIN: Well, the wolf wanted to eat the bird and the duck.

TYRONE: No, that's not right. The wolf wasn't really bad; he was just hungry.

MARIANNA: If he had food, he wouldn't want to eat them. So they took him to the zoo so he could get food.

MS. ELIZABETH: Was there anyone else bad in the story or who didn't do something right?

STUDENTS: (*in unison*) NO!

EVA: Well, Peter's grandfather didn't want him to go into the woods alone, and he did. He didn't listen.

MS. ELIZABETH: Why do you think the grandfather didn't want him to go into the woods alone?

JOVANNA: Well in the woods, even if an animal isn't bad, when it is hungry, it doesn't know anything else to do but eat something. So if there are wild animals around, children shouldn't go alone.

MS. ELIZABETH: So was Peter good or bad?

DARREN: Well, he wasn't really a bad boy, but he didn't listen and he almost got into a lot of trouble.

MS. ELIZABETH: Even though it turned out OK, this story has an important lesson. We need to listen to parents, grandparents, or other grownups who know about danger so we don't get hurt. Did anyone ever do something they were told not to do?

STUDENTS: (*in unison*) No.

MS. ELIZABETH: Are you sure?

SARA: I did. My mommy told me to sit down to drink my milk and hold my cup up so the milk wouldn't spill. I didn't listen and walked around with my milk and I didn't pay attention and it went all over the place. Splat! It made a mess. She didn't get mad; she just said I had to help her clean it up. It was hard work.

Interactive discussions as a result of storybook reading generate problem solving, critical thinking, and emotional responses in preschool children.

CREATIVE STORYTELLING IN THE LITERACY CENTER

Storytelling has a power that reading aloud does not, for it frees the storyteller to use creative techniques. It also has the advantage of keeping the storyteller close to the audience. Telling a story produces an immediate response from children and is one of the surest ways to establish a rapport with young children. Long pieces of literature can be condensed for preschool audiences so that a story can be told in a single sitting. Considered an art, storytelling can be mastered by most people.

When telling a story, it is not necessary to memorize the words, but be sure you know the story well. Learn the catchphrases and quotes that are important to the story. Using an expressive voice enlivens your presentation, but do not let your dramatic techniques overshadow the story itself. Look directly at the children and take their attention into consideration. Have the original book at hand when you have finished telling a story so that the children can enjoy the story again through pictures and printed text (Ritchie, James-Szanton, & Howes, 2002).

Storytelling has a power that reading aloud does not; it frees the storyteller to use creative techniques. It also has the advantage of keeping the storyteller close to the audience. Telling a story produces an immediate response from children and is one of the surest ways to establish a rapport between the listeners and the storyteller. Storytelling is an art that can be mastered by most people.

Creative techniques help storytelling come alive. They excite the imagination, involve the listeners, and motivate children to try storytelling themselves. Take clues for creative techniques from the story. For example, some stories are perfect for the felt-board, others lend themselves to the use of puppets, and still others can be presented as chalk talks, stories told with drawings on the chalkboard.

Felt-Boards

Felt-boards with story characters are a popular and important tool in a classroom. You can purchase felt-board story characters or make your own by drawing figures on construction paper and covering them with clear contact paper or laminate. Attach strips of felt or sandpaper to the backs of the cutouts so they cling to the felt-board. Narrative and informational texts with a limited number of events and characters are best for felt-board retelling.

Puppets

Puppets are used with stories rich in dialogue. There are many kinds of puppets, including finger, hand, stick, and face puppets. Shy children often feel secure telling stories with puppets. Stories such as *The Gingerbread Boy* (Galdone, 1983) and *The Little Red Hen* (Galdone, 1985) are ideal for retelling with puppets because they are short, have few characters, and repeat dialogue. Informational books also can be retold using a puppet.

Music and Sound Effects

Music can be used to accompany almost any story. Music and sounds add interest to storytime. You and the children can use rhythm, voice, and musical instruments to provide sound effects for stories. When preparing to tell a story, first select those parts of the story for which sound effects will be used. Then decide on each sound to be made and who will make it. As the story is told, each person can chime in with his or her assigned sounds. Record the presentation, and then leave the recording in the literacy center with the original book for the children to listen to later. Books that work well with sound effects include *Too Much Noise* (McGovern, 1992), *Five Little Monkeys Reading in Bed* (Christelow, 2011), and *Mr. Brown Can Moo! Can You?* (Dr. Seuss, 1970).

Props

To add a visual element to storytelling, collect stuffed animals, toys, and other articles that represent characters and objects in a story. Display the props at appropriate times during the storytelling. For example, three stuffed bears and a blonde-haired doll can be used as props for *Goldilocks and the Three Bears* (Brett, 1992) and several toy trains can be used as props for *The Little Engine That Could* (Piper, 2001). All of the objects in *There Was an Old Lady Who Swallowed Some Books!* (Colandro, 2012) are easily obtainable, making this book perfect for incorporating props that children can later use to retell this humorous tale.

Chalk Talks

Chalk talks are another technique that attracts listeners. The storyteller draws the story while telling it. Chalk talks are most effective when done with a large chalkboard so that the entire story can be drawn in sequence from beginning to end. Stories can also be drawn on mural paper, using crayons or felt-tip markers instead of chalk. Choose a story with simple illustrations. Draw only a select few pictures as you tell the story. There are stories that have been written as chalk talks, such as *Harold and the Purple Crayon* (Johnson, 1981) and its sequels.

Recorded Stories

Headsets with recorded stories enable children to listen to the story on the headset as they follow along in the text. They are helpful for English language learners because they provide a model for correct English and fluent reading. Have parents and other classroom volunteers make tape recordings of favorite stories.

Electronic Storybooks

Some excellent children's books have been published in an electronic format. The text is read aloud as images move on the screen. Because these stories are animated, they are motivating to children and enhance early literacy skills. Another advantage of electronic books is that skill activities are embedded within storybook reading (Wepner & Ray, 2000). Electronic stories can be projected on a screen for the entire class or listened to alone or with a peer, independent of the teacher.

Children have a great deal of control over the electronic storybook. They can determine the pace of the story presentation and when the pages are turned. They can select a story to read and reread. The story can be programmed to be read word by word or line by line. Children can interact with characters in the book by labeling illustrations, and words spoken by the child can immediately become animated text. Some software story programs allow children to change the story line as the story is being told. Other programs enable young children and adults to create their own books. These books can be personalized and include photos of

family members, pets, the children's homes, and so on. They can include predictable and repetitive phrases so that young children can read their own books. A
child might compose a story like the following about a pet:

> My dog likes his dog food.
>
> My dog likes people food.
>
> My dog likes to play.
>
> My dog likes me.

In addition to building literacy skills, reading electronic storybooks and creating personalized books helps children gain self-esteem as they choose among the
many options in software programs (McKenna, 2001). See Appendix C for more
storytelling ideas.

MODELING STORYTELLING TECHNIQUES

This list of storytelling techniques is far from exhaustive. You and the children will
discover many other ways to tell stories. When you model storytelling strategies
for children, they become motivated to tell stories themselves. After a storytelling
session, children can tell the story you modeled with one of the techniques you
used. Preschoolers will create stories spontaneously with a puppet or with felt-
board story figures.

Engaging in storytelling is an important experience for children. When children tell stories in a presentation manner, as they do with felt-board story characters, they demonstrate their comprehension of the text. They talk about the details
of a story, the main idea, the story events, and the resolution. They interpret voices
of characters as they tell the story. In the following vignette, one author, Lesley,
recalls a successful felt-board activity from her preschool teaching experience.

"When I taught preschool, I wanted the children to learn to use the felt-board
to tell and retell stories. I decided to model using the felt-board by sharing an
easily adaptable, highly predictable story with the class.

"The name of the story was 'A Bunny Named Pat,' an anonymous tale
about a gray bunny who does not like his color because it is so plain. Pat is
able to change his color, but each time he does, he has an unpleasant adventure. The story features the following refrain: 'I'm a bunny named Pat/I'm
sassy and fat/and I can change my color, just like that.'

"When I introduced the story to the children, I asked them to listen for
the different colors that Pat becomes and the problems he faces each time. I
then told the story, using the different-colored bunny characters on the felt-
board. When the story was over, we discussed Pat and his different colors. We
also discussed the ending of the story and its meaning, trying to relate it to the

experiences of the children. I asked children if they ever wanted to be anyone other than themselves, and if so, why.

"After the discussion, I asked the children to think of another color that Pat could become and devise a new adventure for the bunny. The children could select a colored bunny from bunny figures of different colors, and then tell about Pat's new color and his adventure. The bunnies were all made of construction paper and had felt strips glued onto the back to make them stick to the felt-board.

"Four-year-old Lindsey shared her story: 'I'm a bunny named Pat, I'm sassy and fat, and I can change my color just like that.' Pat made himself red like an apple. Some bees was coming. They saw Pat in the red color and they were thinking that Pat was an apple. The bees went near Pat, they wanted to eat him. Pat ran and ran but the bees went after him. So he said, 'Being red is not so good, I'm a bunny called Pat, I am sassy and fat, and I can change my color, just like that.'"

This activity involved children in discussing and creating a story. The experience is motivating because it actively involves the children with the story. The theme of the story, self-image, is an important topic for conversation and can help children understand one another's strengths, weaknesses, and needs. The following section presents instructions for using a felt-board to share "A Bunny Named Pat" in the classroom.

1. Create five identical felt-board bunny characters each of a different color: gray, blue, yellow, green, and orange. As you tell the story below, hold up and place a new colored bunny on the felt-board as each bunny is named. The children can retell the story with the felt characters on their own. They will enjoy the repetition and it will enhance their comprehension of the story.
2. Use the felt-board characters as you tell the story.

"A Bunny Named Pat" (an Anonymous Tale)

Once upon a time there was a little gray bunny and his name was Pat. One day he looked around and saw that all his brothers and sisters, cousins, and friends were gray, too. He thought he would like to be different from them. So he said,

"I'm a bunny called Pat, I'm sassy and fat,

And I can change my color—just like that." (Snap fingers.)

And suddenly Pat was a blue bunny. He was blue like the sky and blue like the sea. He was blue like the twilight and blue like the dawn. It felt nice and cool to be blue. He decided to take a look at himself in the pond. He hurried to the edge and admired his reflection in the water. He leaned over so far that . . . SPLASH! He fell into the pond. Pat fell deep into the blue water and he couldn't swim. He was frightened. He called for help. His friends heard him, but when they came to the pond they couldn't see him because he was blue just like the water. Fortunately a turtle swam by and helped Pat get safely to shore. Pat thanked the turtle. He decided that he didn't like being blue. So he said,

"I'm a bunny called Pat, I'm sassy and fat,

And I can change my color—just like that." (Snap fingers.)

And this time, what color did he change himself to? Yes, he was yellow—yellow like the sun, yellow like a daffodil, yellow like a canary bird. Yellow seemed like such a happy color to be. He was very proud of his new color, and he decided to take a walk through the jungle. Who do you think he met in the jungle? He met the lion and the tiger. The lion and the tiger looked at Pat's yellow fur and said, "What are you doing in that yellow coat? We are the only animals in this jungle that are supposed to be yellow." And they growled so fiercely that Pat the bunny was frightened and he ran all the way home. He said,

"I'm a bunny called Pat, I'm sassy and fat,

And I can change my color—just like that." (Snap fingers.)

And this time, what did he change his color to? Yes, he was green. He was green like the grass and the leaves of the trees. He was green like a grasshopper and like the meadow. As a green bunny, Pat thought he'd be the envy of all the other bunnies. He wanted to play with his other friends in the meadow. Since he was the color of the grass in the meadow, he could not be seen and his friends just ran and jumped about him, not seeing him at all or mistaking him for a grasshopper. So Pat the bunny had no one to play with while he was green. Being green wasn't much fun. So he said,

"I'm a bunny called Pat, I'm sassy and fat,

And I can change my color—just like that." (Snap fingers.)

And what color was he then? Right, he was orange. He was orange like a carrot, a sunset, orange like a pumpkin—he was the brightest color of all. He decided he would go out and play with all his brothers and sisters and friends. But what do you suppose happened? When his friends saw him, they all stopped playing and started to laugh, "Ha-ha, whoever heard of an orange bunny?" No one wanted to play with him. He didn't want to be orange anymore. He didn't want to be a blue bunny because if he fell into the pond, no one could see him to save him. He didn't want to be a yellow bunny and be frightened by the lion and the tiger. He didn't want to be a green bunny because then he was just like the meadow and none of his friends could see him. He said,

"I'm a bunny called Pat, I'm sassy and fat,

And I can change my color—just like that." (Snap fingers.)

Do you know what color Pat the bunny changed himself into this time? Yes, you're right. He changed himself back to gray. And now that he was gray, all of his friends played with him. No one growled or laughed at him. He was gray like a rain cloud, gray like an elephant, gray like pussy willows. It felt warm and comfortable being gray. From that time on, Pat the bunny was always happy being gray, and he decided that it's really best being just what you are.

Refer to Appendix C for sample storytelling techniques.

INDEPENDENT READING TIME

Designate about 10 minutes each day for children to look at or read books in the literacy center. During this time, children can select books they would like to look at and read alone or with a peer. To help children become engaged in independent reading, offer an appealing selection of books on a special shelf, in a basket, or in a plastic crate. Limit the number of books to make the selection process quick and easy (Ritchie et al., 2002). For example, if you have 16 children in your classroom, 25 to 30 books would be appropriate for the independent reading shelf. Provide books that relate to the current topic of study in your classroom. If children are learning about animals, for example, you might select animal books to place in the independent reading basket or on the independent reading shelf. Also include a few books that are already familiar to the children, such as those that have been read aloud by the teacher (Morrow, 1990, 1992, 2015; Morrow, O'Connor, & Smith, 1990). At the end of an independent reading period, invite a few children to tell about the books they looked at or read. By discussing books in this way, children begin to learn accountability. They discover that they need to think about what they are reading as they read.

Literacy Center Time

Literacy center time enables children to choose from several activities involving books and related materials. It is a more active time than independent reading, when only quiet book reading takes place. Children can look at books and use story-related manipulative materials. Before any of these are used by children, the materials need to be modeled by the teacher. In the beginning, the teacher can assign activities for children; once they become familiar with the center materials, the children may select activities themselves. At the literacy center, children participate in reading and writing activities independently and practice important literacy skills. Teachers can alternate having independent reading and literacy center activity time each day. The center time should last for about 15 minutes.

The Teacher's Role
during Independent Reading

Besides preparing the literacy center environment, the teacher also plays an important role before and during independent reading and literacy center time. He or she models activities, helps children select and start using materials, and participates in the children's activities when they need assistance. One of the reasons for independent reading and literacy center time is to engage children in self-directed activities; these are important behaviors to learn.

REACTIONS TO LITERACY CENTERS

A study was carried out in which preschool teachers and children were interviewed from classrooms where they had literacy centers and literacy center time (Morrow, 1992). This was done to determine their attitudes toward having the centers and center time in their classrooms. Teachers commented that the designing of a space for the literacy center demonstrated to the children that books were important in their classroom. Teachers agreed that children were attracted to the area by the manipulative materials in the center, such as the felt-board stories and puppets. They found that the rocking chair, rug, pillows, and stuffed animals made the center relaxing and comfortable for reading. One teacher remarked, "The literacy center became a place where children sat together and shared books. This social context provided a warm atmosphere. The children looked forward to their time there each day." A child commented, "I liked to snuggle on the pillows with a book." Another child commented, "I like to sit in the rocking chair and read." Still another said, "I like to take books home from school."

EVALUATING LITERACY CENTER TIME

Teachers should observe their class to notice which children need help getting started on a task and what activities the children choose to participate in (Morrow, 2015). Techniques for evaluating literacy center time include observing and recording anecdotes of children's literacy activities and making audiotapes and videotapes of children engaged in activities in the literacy center. The evaluation form in Figure 3.3 provides a means for assessing your literacy center.

ASSESSING CHILDREN'S ATTITUDES TOWARD BOOKS

Observing children's behavior while they are listening to stories, reading, or looking at books is an effective method for assessing their attitudes toward books. How much attention do children give to the books they are looking at or reading? Do they simply browse? Do they flip through the pages quickly, paying little attention to print or pictures? Do they demonstrate sustained attention to pictures throughout the book? Note how frequently children choose to look at books when given a range of options. Use occasional one-on-one interviews to ask children what they like to do best in school and at home to determine their interest in reading. During parent–teacher conferences, ask parents if their children voluntarily look at books or pay close attention when they are read to. Also ask parents how often they read to their children. Gather facts about the home literacy environment that will help you understand the child's attitude toward literacy activities. A checklist for assessing attitudes toward reading (see Figure 3.4) can be photocopied and placed in a child's assessment portfolio.

Evaluating Your Literacy Center and Literacy Center Time

_____ Children participate in some phase of the library corner design (develop rules, select a name for the area, develop materials, etc.).

_____ The area is placed in a quiet section of the room.

_____ The area is visually and physically accessible.

_____ Part of the area is partitioned off from the rest of the room.

_____ Bookshelves are available for storing books with spines facing outward.

_____ Open-faced bookshelves are available for new or featured books.

_____ There is an organizational system for shelving books (e.g., baskets by genre).

_____ Five to eight books are available per child.

_____ Many books are available representing three or four levels of difficulty and of the following types:

    _____ picture storybooks

    _____ traditional literature

    _____ poetry

    _____ realistic literature

    _____ informational or expository texts

    _____ biographies

    _____ easy-to-read books

    _____ riddle and joke books

    _____ participation books

    _____ series books

    _____ textless books

    _____ TV-related books

    _____ brochures

    _____ newspapers

    _____ magazines

_____ New books are circulated once a month.

_____ There is a checkout system for children to take home books.

(continued)

FIGURE 3.3. Evaluation checklist for a literacy center.

_____ There is a rug.

_____ There are throw pillows or beanbag chairs.

_____ There is a rocking chair.

_____ There are headsets and taped stories.

_____ There are computers.

_____ There are posters about reading.

_____ There are stuffed animals.

_____ The area is labeled with a name selected by the class.

_____ There are a flannelboard and story characters, along with related books.

_____ There are puppets and props for storytelling.

_____ There are letters of the alphabet.

_____ There are materials for writing stories and making them into books.

_____ There is a private spot in the corner, such as a box to crawl into and read.

_____ The area utilizes about 10% of the classroom; five or six children can fit easily.

FIGURE 3.3. *(continued)*

Child's Name: _____	Date: _____		
Voluntarily looks at or reads books at school.	Always	Sometimes	Never
Asks to be read to.	Always	Sometimes	Never
Listens attentively while being read to.	Always	Sometimes	Never
Responds during book discussions with classmates.	Always	Sometimes	Never
Comments on stories read aloud.	Always	Sometimes	Never
Takes books home to read voluntarily.	Always	Sometimes	Never
Teacher Comments:			

FIGURE 3.4. Checklist for assessing attitudes toward reading.

Young children are eager to learn and be introduced to new ideas. Books with nonfiction stories provide a wealth of information for children, who can have real and vicarious experiences through the stories.

CONCLUSION

This chapter has focused on literacy centers and activities that integrate language, play, content, reading, and writing. As preschool educators, we hope to inspire children to become lifelong voluntary readers. When books are celebrated in literacy centers and activities, young children are more likely to develop a positive attitude toward reading. In addition to read-alouds and other teacher-led activities, children need time to explore books and storytelling materials alone and with peers. With careful planning, teachers can help children make effective use of time and materials in literacy centers that foster a love of language, reading, and writing.

Preschool in Practice

Making Words

Literacy centers offer an approach to learning and classroom organization that facilitates individualization of instruction and encourages independence in learning. Centers can enhance skill development and can be used to provide reinforcement activities for children following teacher-directed instruction.

A Making Words literacy center gives children an independent activity that promotes spelling and reading. The materials needed for construction of a Making Words center include construction paper, pictures representing multisyllabic words (*elephant*, *helicopter*, *watermelon*, etc.), and letter cards. The pictures are glued to the construction paper and the word is written below the picture. In a plastic sandwich baggie, place letter cards with the individual letters, for example, *e-l-e-p-h-a-n-t*. The construction paper with the picture and word, along with the sandwich baggie with the letters, can be stored in a large zip-lock plastic baggie.

Children will be able to read the word using the picture clue. Then they use the individual letter cards to make other words, as in the example in Figure 3.5.

Literacy Center: Alphabet Bingo

Alphabet Bingo can help children identify letters of the alphabet. The game can be played by small groups of children with one child serving as the "caller" for the other children. The materials needed include premade Bingo cards using letters of the alphabet, small individual letter cards (for the caller), and Bingo markers such as bottle caps or dried lima beans. Ready-made alphabet Bingo cards and letters can be downloaded from *www.mcedservices.com/ESL/ Bingo/AlphBing.pdf.*

| e | l | e | p | h | a | n | t |

| p | e | t |

| h | a | t |

FIGURE 3.5. Example of a Making Words activity using *elephant*.

The steps for Alphabet Bingo include the following:

1. The caller gives each player an Alphabet Bingo card and markers.
2. The caller puts the individual letter cards in a bowl and mixes them up.
3. Picking out one letter card at a time, the caller calls out the letter name and holds up the card to help other children with letter identification.
4. If a player has the letter on their alphabet Bingo card, they cover it with a marker.
5. The first player to cover one row of letters on the card gets Alphabet Bingo.

The Alphabet Bingo game can be played using uppercase letters and can be used to help children match lowercase and uppercase letters. In addition, it can be used to match rhyming words.

Learning to Work in Literacy Centers

Teachers usually schedule literacy center time a few times each week for about 30–40 minutes each time. During each period children choose an activity and decide with whom they will work. One important goal for literacy centers is to help children become independent learners. Therefore, it is helpful to develop some class rules for working in literacy centers. Below is a chart developed by a first-grade teacher and her class:

Working in Literacy Centers
1. Choose a literacy center.
2. Decide whom you will work with or if you will work alone.
3. Decide where you will work.
4. Try activities you have not done before.
5. Try working with someone you haven't worked with before.

6. Speak softly—others are working.
7. Keep the literacy center neat.
8. Keep the literacy center materials together.
9. When you finish, return the materials to the literacy center.
10. Record completed activities in your log.

CHILDREN'S LITERATURE CITED IN THIS CHAPTER

Dinosaur Thunder by Marion Dane Bauer (2012). Scholastic.
Five Little Monkeys Reading in Bed by Eileen Christelow (2011). Clarion Books.
The Gingerbread Boy by Paul Galdone (1983). Houghton Mifflin Harcourt.
Goldilocks and the Three Bears by Jan Brett (1992). Putnam's.
Harold and the Purple Crayon by Crockett Johnson (1981). HarperCollins.
How Do Dinosaurs Play with Their Friends? by Jane Yolen (2006). Scholastic.
The Little Engine That Could by Watty Piper (2001). Penguin Young Readers Group.
The Little Red Hen by Paul Galdone (1985). Houghton Mifflin Harcourt.
Mr. Brown Can Moo! Can You? by Dr. Seuss (1970). Random House. *Peter and the Wolf* by Sergei Prokofiev (1986). Puffin Books.
Peter's Chair by Ezra Jack Keats (1998). Puffin Books.
Pierre by Maurice Sendak (1991). HarperCollins.
The Tale of Peter Rabbit by Beatrix Potter (2002). Warne.
There Was an Old Lady Who Swallowed Some Books! by Lucille Colandro (2012). Cartwheel Books.
The Three Little Pigs by Paul Galdone (1984). Houghton Mifflin Harcourt.
Too Much Noise by Ann McGovern (1992). Houghton Mifflin Harcourt.
Where the Wild Things Are by Maurice Sendak (1963). Harper & Row.

IDEAS FOR DISCUSSION, REFLECTION, AND ACTION

1. Create a real or imagined space for a literacy center in your classroom. Make a sketch and list the materials needed. Take inventory of what you have and what you need. Figure out the cost to make it the type of center you would like it to be.

2. A literacy center library needs multiple genres of children's literature. Sort the books in your classroom into genre piles, and count how many genres you have in your room. How many are informational and how many are narratives? Make a list of books you want to add. Visit classrooms of other teachers in your building to see what their literacy centers look like so you can share ideas.

3. This chapter presents many ideas and materials for use in the literacy center. What other materials would you create for your literacy center? Explain the purpose of the material, how you created it, and how you use it.

4. Many ways to share stories with children are mentioned in this chapter, including using digital stories and storytelling techniques such as puppets and props. Do you think these extra effects are helpful, or is it best not to tamper with a book and just *read* it?

CHAPTER 4

Nurturing Young Children's Language and Conversational Skills

Kathy and Tylea (4-year-olds) are drawing bugs around a tall tree on a mural in progress about spring. The teacher helps the girls get started, saying, "Maybe the ants go down here in the soil." She points to the area beneath the tree. Kathy is drawing a snail while Tylea sketches ants.

> KATHY: I can write *ant* by that . . . there you go. I did it for you.
>
> TYLEA: What's your next writing?
>
> KATHY: I don't know. Another ant. I'll write that here. I can do it.
>
> TYLEA: I'm gonna make my ant blue. I'm gonna make a butterfly behind the snail.

KATHY: Look! I found the snail in the bug book. Do you like my snail? Isn't it cute? Now next is gonna be a spider. Spiders come out, too.

TYLEA: Eeeek! I don't like spiders. They're crawley. I already drawed one down here.

Notice how Kathy and Tylea use language to talk about language—in this case, writing the word *ant* on the mural. They name animals and insects—butterfly, snail, spider—and they use descriptive language, like *crawley*.

Creating a supportive learning environment where young children can work, play, and learn with understanding and joy is the sine qua non of effective preschool practice. It is absolutely essential for ensuring children's oral language development and for establishing a permanent connection between oral language abilities and emerging early literacy skills. Children succeed when they are provided with learning conditions that nurture their language discoveries, their different uses of language, and their first attempts to read and write. When you create a supportive learning environment for talk you also create opportunities for children to learn together about the real world and about possible worlds; where they can discover the uses of their minds, imagination, materials, and new technologies; and where they can feel a part of a friendly (and smart) community.

ENGAGING CONVERSATIONAL STRATEGIES

Substantive conversation is a form of talk adults can use to engage children in long and rich dialogues about important topics. The need for such conversation between adults and children and among children is very great, driven by a basic human need to know; to tell; and to explain about yourself, your experiences, and the world around you. How can teachers routinely stimulate substantive talk with the children in their preschool classrooms? Rich talk and compelling themes are two top-notch ways to encourage substantive talk more often in the classroom setting (Dangel & Durden, 2010). Opportunities for rich, extended dialogues on content-rich topics build up children's expressive and receptive vocabularies—and vocabulary acquisition is at the heart of language development.

Rich Talk

One way to ensure a lot of substantive conversation is to stimulate talk that is rich with ideas, facts, observations, connections, and feelings that relate to children's immediate experiences. This is often easier said than done in the preschool classroom. Managing groups of young children in classroom space can preclude long and rich dialogues in quiet, intimate places where conversations can go on at length. Recall all those "one shots," or short exchanges, about clean-up, wash-up, and line-up that so often occur in the course of the preschool day. Yet despite these realities, rich talk can be supported in different activities that make up the preschooler's day. Children are more likely to engage in rich talk, for example, when engaged in familiar routines and activities. Familiarity with what they are doing frees them to give their attention to talking about what they are doing—in other words, they are able to use language over action. Therefore, routine activities are fertile ground for engendering rich talk between children.

Rich talk is also more likely to occur in dramatic play. This activity presses children to use language to imagine, to negotiate roles, to describe actions, and to explain the rules of play. For example, in the following play scenario, several children are running a flower shop and negotiate their roles in the shop.

> The play starts with a short disagreement about whether the shop is open or closed, but the children eventually decide that it's open. The following takes place between two boys:
>
> BOY 1: OK. It's open. Order something. Some prette-e-e-e flowers.
>
> BOY 2: I don't wanna be the person buying flowers all the time.
>
> BOY 1: OK, fine. You can be the cash register guy—over here. (*Motions behind the counter.*)
>
> BOY 2: Then you can buy the roses, the daisies, and stuff. OK?
>
> BOY 1: I'd like to place an order for flowers, please.
>
> BOY 2: OK, what do you want? The roses? The daisies? These pretty purple ones here?
>
> BOY 1: I wanna buy some flowers for my wife. Here's the money. She's over there.
>
> BOY 2: (*to his assistant*) All right, we need flowers for the wife. Make it roses . . . the redder ones.
>
> BOY 1: Thanks. Keep the change.

Small-group activities and one-to-one interactions between adults and children offer many opportunities for rich talk. This is especially so when the activities have a clear goal and adult talk is contingent on the child's talk as in the following exchange between Sam and his dad at an air show. As Sam and his dad look skyward they see a number of airplanes in flight. The air show announcer says, "Jake Roberts is flying a biplane today!"

> SAM: Which one is the biplane?
>
> DAD: See the plane that has two sets of wings?

SAM: I see! I see! One pair right on top of the other.

DAD: Yes, the two sets of wings are stacked one on top of the other.

SAM: Why are they called biplanes?

DAD: Well, *bi* can mean two—the airplane has two sets of wings so it is called a biplane. Can you find another biplane in the sky?

SAM: Over there, I see a red one—it's a red biplane.

Conversational Strategies

Good conversation is an art. It is especially the case when adults seek to have substantive conversations with young children that invite them to talk along and listen with comprehension. There is a science to having good conversations with young children that teachers can learn. From research we know of several effective talk strategies that can make the difference between many good conversations between teachers and children, and not having so many.

The following sections explore three conversation strategies that should be a part of every preschool teacher's communication skills repertoire: (1) clarify–extend, (2) question–tell, and (3) think-aloud.

Clarify–Extend

Research tells us that when adults define words, when they clarify confusing ideas and terms, and when they add details to conversations, children learn more language and are exposed to more new words (Bloom, 2002). Here's how it works:

- Listen to what a child says.
- Pick up on an idea from the child's talk.
- Add to it, explain it further, and disentangle any confusion.

The following example illustrates how a teacher clarified and extended what the child said:

CHILD: It was hot in here and that made all the water vaporate and that vaporation makes flowers droop.

TEACHER: Yes, water evaporates from the soil when it's hot, and then the plant doesn't have enough. It wilts or droops.

Question–Tell

Research supports asking questions and telling answers as effective ways to interact with young children so long as these talk strategies are contingent or built upon the child's interests and efforts (Test, Cunningham, & Lee, 2010; Wood, McMahon, & Cranstoun, 1980). Here's how it works:

- Join the child in an activity.
- Draw attention to parts and details.
- Maintain interest with talk contingent on the child's effort.
- Offer praise and encouragement.

Consider the following example in which the teacher helps Simon complete a puzzle (Wood et al., 1980):

SIMON: Are there pieces missing here?

TEACHER: You'll have to start the right way up. You have to get them all turned over the right way.

STEPHANIE: Can I do this?

TEACHER: You can do that one, Stephanie, yes. I put this out for a little girl.

STEPHANIE: I'm a big girl.

TEACHER: Oh! You are a big girl. I'm sorry.

SIMON: Does this go at the top?

TEACHER: Yes, Simon. Look at the top of that clock again and that's the one that comes right at the very top. Look at the big hands on it. Can you see? Right, start off with that, all right?

SIMON: This at the top.

TEACHER: No, that one comes next, doesn't it?

SIMON: Then . . . then that one goes in there and the one goes there!

TEACHER: That's right. Now you've got the idea.

SIMON: That goes there.

TEACHER: Good boy.

SIMON: I am doing very much.

TEACHER: You're doing very much. That must be because you're 4 now, right?

SIMON: Yes.

Stephanie, as you will likely have observed, does not need any help because she is a "big girl." Note, too, the contingent uses of language by the teacher. She *tells* relevant information in response to the children's questions. She *asks* leading questions, such as "Right, start off with that, all right?" And she provides immediate feedback: "No, that one comes next, doesn't it?"

Think-Aloud

A think-aloud is just that: a time when adults say what they are thinking as they do something or consider a problem. Adults instill a sense of inquiry in children when they frequently show their own thinking and wonder about things around them. When they model curiosity and think aloud, they expose children to the abstract uses of language, such as imagining, and demonstrate an attitude of learning (Tough, 1981). Here are the essential steps for using the think-aloud procedure:

- Involve the child in what you are doing.
- Verbalize your thoughts.
- Model how to think through a task or problem to a conclusion.

Consider the following example. Pay attention to how the teacher talks about what she is thinking, as in, "You know, I can observe this apple with all my five senses." She then continues to "think aloud" as she describes the attributes of the apple:

> Ms. Marci is using circle time to introduce the children to the vocabulary and methods of observe, predict, check in science. She shows them an apple and says, "You know I can observe this apple with all my five senses. I can see that it is red. I can feel that it is smooth on the surface. It's not a cold thing and it's not a hot thing. I can shake it, but it does not make a sound—none at all. But, you know what? I cannot see inside the apple right now. So I can only predict what is inside—maybe white stuff and seeds. How can I check that out, I wonder?" She then asks the children how they might check out her predictions.

Compelling Themes

Another means of bringing about substantive conversation in your preschool classroom is the deliberate use of compelling themes. A theme-based approach is certainly not new to early childhood education, but our intentions can be fresh and new. A 21st-century goal is to use themes that strengthen and build children's word and world knowledge. For this we need compelling themes that organize experiences, activities, projects, and play around strong early learning standards in language arts, mathematics, science, social studies, the creative arts, and health.

In the vignette below you will find an exemplary illustration of the use of a compelling theme in Ben Mardell's preschool classroom during their squirrel unit (Mardell, 1999).

> Step inside Ben's preschool classroom. Hear the excitement as the children get ready to become squirrel scientists for the next 4 weeks. Today the

children are getting ready to go on a daily walk around the neighborhood to create their squirrel census. Their goal? Count all the squirrels they can spot.

On the walk they talk about squirrels and Ben talks to them about different colors of squirrels as well as their habits. Another day the children and their teacher gather in a classroom "squirrel lab" to think about what squirrels eat. Aviva wonders if squirrels eat snakes, but Shoshanna and Jessie vehemently disagree!

Ben also introduces the class to a scientific drawing of a squirrel with labels. He asks the children to make their own observational drawings and learn about the heart, the lungs, the stomach, and of course the bushy tail.

Across the 4 weeks these students read squirrel stories, draw and write squirrel books and silly squirrel stories, and even watch a real squirrel scientist, Judy, from the Natural History Museum as she shows the internal anatomy of a squirrel specimen. Ben's preschool squirrel scientists have become squirrel experts in this compelling theme that includes science, the environment, problem solving and reflection, writing, reading, and even number sense. Who wouldn't want to be a scientist after exploring this theme?

Four features of the squirrel unit transform it from an ordinary learning experience to a robust one that develops content knowledge, therefore making it a compelling theme.

1. *It is content-rich.* It incorporates concepts, facts, and skills from a variety of content areas. It addresses a full range of early learning standards and provides many varied opportunities for learning, especially in science.
2. *It is engaging.* This theme interests and excites these children, who are tremendously curious about their world and knowledge seekers about living things in their immediate surroundings.
3. *It is enduring.* Through its activities, projects, and play, children are exposed to powerful disciplinary ideas that they can remember and use later on in future learning, such as keen observation, careful drawing, and accurate labeling.
4. *It is thoughtful.* The theme challenges children's thinking and stretches their skills to new levels. It supports intellectual achievement.

PLANNING FOR PLAY

Based on research, play is a satisfying activity for young children where they can practice and extend what they know. Play pulls forward children's physical, emotional, social, and cognitive development to higher levels of performance (Lobman

& O'Neill, 2011; Bodrova & Leong, 2007; Johnson et al., 2005). At age 3, children who engaged in more pretend talk during play were more likely to perform well on assessments of receptive vocabulary and narrative production (Cunningham & Zibulsky, 2014; Dickinson & Tabors, 2001; Johnson et al., 2005; Neuman & Roskos, 2007; Singer & Singer, 1990). There also are strong links between dramatic play and long-term language growth (Dickinson & Tabors, 2001; McGee & Richgels, 2012). Play, therefore, is an essential best practice in the early childhood classroom.

Children should be in charge of their own play often—otherwise, from their point of view, it just isn't play. Yet, at the same time, they need guidance and structure for successful and satisfying play. As an early childhood educator, you should be guiding children toward mature play behaviors by the onset of kindergarten. Mature play is not simple play that consists of single actions and mimicry. Nor is it sequenced play where children assume a familiar role, follow a simple sequence of events, and use pretend props. Mature play is more complex; it asks children to (1) create an imaginary situation; (2) use objects in a symbolic way; (3) use language to enact play; (4) take on explicit roles; and (5) listen, understand, and follow rules. Dramatic play provides a highly motivating context for children to develop these more advanced play skills.

Teachers implement dramatic play best practice when they (1) link potential play topics to current curriculum themes; (2) build children's background for play talk and roles (e.g., through real and virtual field trips); (3) involve children in setting up the dramatic play area relevant to a specific theme (e.g., post office, travel agency, veterinarian's office); (4) introduce new words, new roles, and new routines that build vocabulary and content knowledge related to the theme; and (5) help children remember their dramatic play episodes, connecting them to the broader learning activities going on in the classroom.

Play is most beneficial for learning when it involves pretending and creating a play story that lasts for an extended period of time. You can enrich the learning power of play when you help children plan for it (Bodrova & Leong, 2007; Soderman, Gregory, & O'Neill, 1999; Umek & Peklaj, 2010). Follow this procedure for play planning:

1. Provide background knowledge for a new play idea by reading to children or going on a field trip.
2. Ask the children to help you change a play setting for the new play theme.
3. On chart paper, print the name of the play theme (e.g., The Kids' Café).
4. Ask children to tell you things that this play setting will need to work. Write down their ideas. Remind children to listen carefully. Someone else may have thought of their idea already. If so, children can put up a thumb so that others know they had that idea too. (You may end here for the day or continue.)

5. Ask the children to suggest where the class might get these items. Note the source next to the items on the list (e.g., Miss Carol's house, Tanya's house, the center, a store).

6. Have the children help you decide how to get the supplies: ask for donations, bring them in from home, and so on. Make decisions about who will bring in the supplies.

7. As the supplies come in, check them off the list. This can be done at the start of playtime or during group time. Have the children help you compose and mail thank-you notes to those who contributed.

8. Meanwhile, ask the children, "What roles do we need for this play idea?" List the roles with a job description for each (e.g., waiter: takes orders, delivers food, tells the cook what to make).

9. With the children's help, set up the play setting during playtime or tell them you will be setting it up and to look for it the next day.

10. As the play begins, move it along by asking questions, such as "How will I know the Café is open?" to motivate reading and writing or by taking a role to model the use of language and introduce new words.

The following is a vignette of a carefully planned play setting and, as a result, the literacy activities that took place:

Ms. Casey has designed a veterinary clinic dramatic play center in her preschool classroom to enrich a unit of study on pets. The classroom veterinary hospital includes a waiting room; chairs; a table filled with magazines, children's literature, and pamphlets about pet care; posters about pets; office hour notices; a "No Smoking" sign; and a sign advising visitors to "Check in with the nurse when arriving." A nurse's desk holds patient forms on clipboards, a telephone, an address and telephone book, appointment cards, a calendar, and a computer for recording appointments and patient records. The examination area features patient folders, prescription pads, white coats, masks, gloves, cotton swabs, a toy doctor's kit, stuffed animals to serve as patients, and an area called the pharmacy for medicine.

Ms. Casey guides children in the use of the various materials in the clinic by reminding the children to read in waiting areas, fill out forms with prescriptions or appointment times, and fill out forms with information about an animal's condition and treatment. In addition to giving directions, Ms. Casey models behaviors by playing with the children whenever new materials are introduced in the play center. For example, while waiting for the doctor to see her stuffed-animal patient, Ms. Casey reads a picture storybook to her puppy, and then reads a magazine herself.

Several children's literacy behaviors were observed in this setting. For example, Jessica waits to see the doctor. She tells her stuffed toy dog, Fluff, not to worry, that the doctor won't hurt him. She asks Jenny, who is waiting with her stuffed toy cat, Muffin, what the kitten's problem is. The girls agonize over the ailments of their pets. After a while they stop talking and Jessica picks up a book from the table and pretends to read *How Do Dinosaurs Eat Their Food?* (Yolen, 2005) to Fluff. Jessica shows Fluff the pictures as she reads.

Jennie runs into the doctor's office shouting, "My dog got runned over by a car!" They go into the doctor's room where he bandages the dog's leg; the two children then decide that the incident must be reported to the police. Before calling the police, they get out the telephone book and turn to a map to find the spot where the dog had been hit. Then, they call the police on the toy phone to report the incident.

Jonah examines Preston's teddy bear and writes a report in the patient's folder. He reads his scribble writing out loud and says, "This teddy bear's blood pressure is 29 points. He should take 62 pills an hour until he is better and keep warm and go to bed." While he reads, he shows Preston what he wrote so he understands what to do. He asks his nurse to type the notes into the computer.

As a result of this play theme the teacher made a word wall of new words discussed during play. This increased both oral language and reading language.

Literacy-Enriched Play Settings

Designing a dramatic play area to match a topic of study makes the content more meaningful for children. Modify the dramatic play center whenever you begin to study a new theme. Be sure to guide and model the use of materials. It can be useful to record literacy behaviors in the play area (Neuman & Roskos, 1989). This will provide information about what children are doing and which play settings stimulate literacy behavior. Assessment of literacy behavior in play settings should be done by the teacher about once a month.

Almost any topic of study can be enhanced with a literacy-enriched play setting. The following are play settings, with suggestions for literacy materials that relate to the theme.

Post Office

Include show boxes, stickers for stamps, envelopes, paper and pencils, baskets to sort different types of mail, and a map to show where mail travels, as well as resource books on related topics.

The Zoo

Provide plastic or stuffed animals, magazines and books about animals, blocks to build cages for the animals, and buttons or foam shapes as food for the animals.

Doctor's Office

Include a telephone, desk, clip boards, paper and pencils, dolls, bandages, posters of the human body, books about nutrition and health, pillows and a bed, and white jackets for doctors.

Supermarket

Supply pretend food, empty cereal and pasta boxes, empty milk cartons, shopping baskets, paper or plastic shopping bags, cash registers, and pretend money. Children can take turns being shoppers and checkout clerks. Give children a list of groceries to buy to encourage word recognition.

WHAT ABOUT ENGLISH LANGUAGE LEARNERS?

Several of these instructional techniques are already popular in the preschool setting and used routinely. Will you need to change the way you think about creating a supportive learning environment for talking, reading, and writing for your English language learners? The answer is not at all. At first, you will likely need to do more of the talking. Don't be discouraged that an English language learner does not respond right away to your attempts at conversation. Remember that initially there is likely to be a nonverbal period for English language learners when they will be trying to make sense of the new language that is being used in the classroom. During that time, they will be getting used to the new sounds of the language and will be beginning to try to understand what different words mean. They will not start using their new language until they feel comfortable that they have something to say and they know the right way to say it. And even after they begin to use their new language, there will be a lot that they won't know how to say.

By carefully setting up everyday conversations, guided participation, and language scaffolds, you will be helping the English language learners, as well as the other children in your classroom. So even if the English language learners aren't using their new language yet, they are developing important information. And when they do start to use their new language all of these techniques will help them to learn more quickly.

TECHNIQUES THAT NURTURE CHILDREN'S LANGUAGE
AND CONVERSATIONAL SKILLS

Much of children's oral language learning occurs through conversations with adults and peers—but not all. To master the less obvious oral language skills that are the foundation of literacy, children need to be given oral language instruction. They need to be taught, for example, to pay attention to how words rhyme, to manipulate morphemes (e.g., plurals), and to listen for main ideas. They need guidance in what to say and when in social situations. At times, preschool instruction in oral language skills should be direct and explicit. But at the same time interactions need to be sensitive, responsive, and playful. This is no easy feat! Fortunately, there are several instructional techniques that are geared to teaching oral language skills to the young child.

The Language Experience Approach

The Language Experience Approach (LEA) is a longtime favorite of both adults and children. First and foremost, LEA values the child's experiences, ideas, and language. A major goal of LEA is to provide children with a rich language environment and many opportunities to articulate their thoughts and ideas (Dorr, 2006). Basically, LEA involves child dictation of a common experience with the adult as the scribe. For example, the following experience was dictated by three children after a field trip to the zoo:

> "We went to the zoo yesterday. There were lots of animals. We saw monkeys, lions, elephants, tigers, and turtles. The monkeys were funny. They jumped all over the place. At the snack shop, we got cotton candy. We had fun!"

Language experience dictation holds a wealth of opportunity for children to use language and to see literacy in action modeled by the adult. Even better, it results in a written text that children can revisit often to remember and try reading on their own. The basic procedure for LEA is outlined in Table 4.1.

Morning Message

Morning Message is an LEA methodology. It will prepare children to construct and understand the meaning of the texts that they later read and to share their ideas with others through talking and writing. According to Hindman and Wasik (2012), there are three essential components of Morning Message: public construction of the message, discussion of the message's code-related content, and discussion of the meaning of the message. With children gathered around the board or chart, the teacher writes the Morning Message in front of children to model the process of writing a message (Essa & Burnham, 2009; Hindman & Wasik, 2012).

- The teacher begins by thinking aloud about what the message should say, demonstrating for the children that the writing process begins with careful consideration of one's own ideas.
- Then the teacher encourages input from the students about what the message should say, taking advantage of opportunities to link the message to children's recent experiences and ongoing classroom units of study.

- The Morning Message should reinforce key vocabulary, ideas, and letters of the alphabet under examination in the curriculum. For example, the teacher calls attention to key words and ideas related to the current unit of study (e.g., "Today we are learning about dolphins") or highlight an important upcoming event (e.g., "Later today we will have a visitor who works at the aquarium").
- Once the message is written, the teacher reads the message aloud at least once, or invites children to read the message if they are able.
- Using the sentences generated for the Morning Message, the teacher can work with small groups of children to discuss the message, including letters, sounds in words, vocabulary, or connections to the classroom curriculum.

TABLE 4.1. The Language Experience Approach

Procedural steps	Explanation
Step 1: *Have a common experience.*	Share a common experience with children, such as a nature walk, field trip, guest presentation, or special event.
Step 2: *Take dictation.*	Ask the children to help you remember the event by writing about it. Have them recall highlights and write their comments on chart paper. Read back each child's contribution, pointing to the printed words. Talk about what the words look like and how they sound. Compliment the children on their word choices.
Step 3: *Read the story.*	Once you have a complete story that captures the common experience (about four or five sentences), read the text to the children. Then read it again and invite the children to read along with you as you reread the piece. Finally, read it one more time. This time, pause to let individual children "read" portions of the story.
Step 4: *Explore the story.*	Now have some fun with the story. Engage children in discovering letters ("Let's find all the *M*'s in this story and circle them with a red marker") or words ("Let's look for that word *geranium*. Remember we saw those beautiful red flowers on our walk"). Help them search and find specific alphabet letters and words. Help them listen for sounds in key words.
Step 5: *Read the story again.*	Post the story on an easel for reading again at a later time. At each return to the story, make instructional points related to oral language comprehension, vocabulary, phonological awareness, and alphabet letters. Provide copies for children to "read" on their own and to take home.

A Morning Message one classroom used was to write the news for their class once a week for a month. These news messages were written at the end of the week since they recorded activities done during that week. Children dictated and the teacher wrote the activity such as "We went to the bakery this week." A child would illustrate about what was written. Children could consider other additions, such as photos or three-dimensional items that might increase interest and add visual detail. Other classes write daily news messages, which should be reviewed periodically since they add up by the end of each week. When the month has passed, assemble the pages into a book. Make a cover (e.g., *The Merry Month of May*). Put it in the library center for children to look at and read on their own.

Sing, Say, Read, and Write Pocket Charts

Songs, rhymes, and poems are an ever-fresh source of delight for young children. These playful ways with words improve children's memory, phonological awareness, vocabulary, and creative uses of language. On occasion you should capture the spirit of songs, rhymes, and poems by writing them down and displaying them in pocket charts for children to sing, say, read, and write on their own. Here's what to do over time:

1. Choose a song verse, chant, nursery rhyme, or short poem.
2. Sing, chant, or say the selection with children. Have them repeat phrases to help them learn the piece.
3. Write the words on sentence strips in front of the children. Say each word as you write the phrases and sentences. Then sing, chant, or say each phrase or sentence as the children watch. Invite them to chime in. Place the strip in the pocket chart. When the entire selection is placed in the chart, sing, chant, or say it through in its entirety while pointing to the words.
4. Have the children close their eyes and mix up the sentence strips. After they open their eyes have them help you put the strips back in order.

Wall Calendar for Daily News

A wall calendar is a good way to enrich your setting with print and provide opportunities for children to talk, read, and write on topics of special interest to them. It also offers a refreshing alternative to the traditional calendar approach because it includes the daily news and increases the number of children who can participate in calendar activities. Follow these steps:

1. Select a wall space for the calendar. You will need enough space to display five 8½″ × 11″ sheets of manila paper, one for each day of the week.
2. During calendar time, have an 8½″ × 11″ sheet of paper ready on a nearby easel.

3. Following your calendar routine, work with the children to record the following information on the manila paper: day of the week, date, weather, and one newsworthy item (e.g., "We are going to the bakery today"). Write the text in large print.

4. Ask for a volunteer or two who will make a drawing for the calendar page at the art table. Talk about what the drawing might be and what colors to use. Be sure to make a note of who is illustrating the page for the day.

5. Collect the calendar page at the end of the day. Consider any other additions, such as photos or three-dimensional items that might increase interest and add visual detail. Attach the page to the wall or a wire in sequence as the days of the week pass.

6. Each day, review the calendar wall with the children. Help them remember past events and recall details for each day. Have them practice remembering the names of the days of the week and counting.

7. Repeat steps 1–6 for each week of the month. If possible, display each week, moving each passing week further up the wall to create a giant calendar of the month. Put a pointer by the calendar so that children can locate specific days and view, read, and remember events that have passed.

8. When the month has passed, assemble the pages into a book. Make a cover and put it in the library center for children to look at and read on their own.

CONCLUSION

This chapter described a number of teaching techniques and activities that nurture young children's language and conversational skills. In addition, key design elements for creating rich oral language environments were highlighted. Children thrive in learning environments that help them use what they already know to make sense of new information, help them build an understanding of acts and ideas, and help them check that their own thinking and actions are in line with the goals of an activity. A classroom environment that nurtures children's language and conversational skills is essential for ensuring oral language development and establishing a permanent connection between oral language abilities and emerging early literacy skills.

Preschool in Practice

Engaging Students in Story Retelling Using Puppets and Felt Figures

Children enjoy hearing teachers tell stories, especially when the storytelling is complemented by the use of props. After hearing (and seeing) the story demonstrated by the teacher, the children can use the puppets or felt figures to retell the story. The familiar story

"I Know an Old Lady Who Swallowed a Fly" lends itself to props and storytelling. The storytelling is as follows:

1. Introduce the story, for example, "I Know an Old Lady Who Swallowed a Fly." The words to this story can be easily found online, including at *http://lyrics.wikia.com/Burl_Ives:I_Know_An_Old_Lady_Who_Swallowed_A_Fly*.

2. As you tell the story, use props that you have printed out or made yourself: the figure of the old lady, the fly, the spider, the bird, the cat, the dog, the cow, and the horse. These figures can be cut out of felt, or you can make puppets to represent the old lady and the animals.

3. After telling the story, discuss the sequence of events, using the old lady and the other figures.

4. Retell the story a second time, using the figures again, and encourage students to tell it along with you. Tell students that the figures help you to remember and retell the story.

5. Encourage children to practice retelling the story on their own, using the "Old Lady" characters. This experience gives children an opportunity to expand and use their oral language, attend to story events and sequencing, and build confidence in their ability to tell a good story.

Let's Describe It!

Having children richly describe common things in their environment can help them become more observant and enhance their ability to use descriptive vocabulary. For this activity, you only need to look around the classroom (or in your bag) to find an object to describe. You may want to post a chart like the one in Figure 4.1 to help children observe various attributes of an object.

First, select a common item to describe. It can be something as simple as a pencil, a tape dispenser, or a tube of lipstick. Take an item, such as the pencil, and tell students you are going to try to describe it.

Describe it!

1. Name
2. Parts
3. Color(s)
4. Smell
5. Feel
6. Shape
7. It is used for . . .

FIGURE 4.1. Let's Describe It! chart.

1. Point to number 1 on the chart and name the object: "This is a pencil."
2. Point to number 2 on the chart as you say, "How many parts does the pencil have?" Be sure to point out that the pencil has lead in the middle, has wood on the outside, a metal rim at the top, and a rubber eraser .Point out that "This pencil has four parts: lead, wood, metal rim, and rubber eraser."
3. Point to number 3 on the chart as you say, "This pencil is yellow on the outside, the wood is beige (or tan), the metal rim is gold, and the eraser is orange (or pink)."
4. Point to number 4 on the chart as you say, "This pencils smells a bit like wood to me."
5. Point to number 5 on the chart as you say, "The wooden part of the eraser is hard, but the eraser feels soft."
6. Point to number 6 on the chart as you say, "This pencil is round, and long and thin. One end is sharp (the point) and the other end is flat."
7. Point to number 7 on the chart as you say, "A pencil is used for writing—and you can use the eraser if you need to make a correction. I could use this pencil to write you a note or letter."

Do this activity with children several times, each time engaging them to elaborate on the description of attributes. When children are familiar with the activity, have them select a partner. Put a number of small items in a bag (hair pin/clip, sun glasses, paper clip, clothes pin, emery board, etc.) and have each pair pull an object out of the bag. Have students take turns describing the object and encourage them to use the class chart to help describe as much as they can about the object.

Children will especially enjoy making this a guessing game. Place one item in a brown bag, have one child come up and look into the bag. The child then uses steps 2–7 on the Describe It! list to describe the item. Children in the class raise their hand when they think they know what item is being described. This activity will help children develop acute observational skills and gives them opportunities to use their oral language abilities to more richly describe the world around them.

Song, Poem, and Nursery Rhyme Chants

Children are always delighted when they "know" and can "chant" a song, a poem, or nursery rhyme on their own. Begin by identifying short songs, poems, and nursery rhymes that may appeal to the children in your classroom and select one to use with your students. In the following example the teacher printed "Hickory, Dickory, Dock" on a large piece of chart paper.

> "Hickory, Dickory, Dock"
> Hickory, dickory, dock,
> The mouse ran up the clock.
> The clock struck one,
> The mouse did run!
> Hickory, dickory, dock.

Read the nursery rhyme to the children the first time, using gestures and pantomime as appropriate. For example, with "Hickory, Dickory, Dock" you can run your fingers upward to indicate "the mouse ran up the clock," make a "dong" sound for "the clock struck one" (dong!), and fingers running downward for "the mouse did run." Then, as you read it a second time, read a line and then have the children "echo" or repeat the line. The third time you read the rhyme ask all the children to read along with you.

You can provide multiple opportunities for children to engage in reading the nursery rhyme by having one side of the group of children read one line and the other side of the group read the next, taking turns. "Hickory, Dickory, Dock" has a title and five lines so you could have the children "count off" 1–6, then have all the 1's read the title, the 2's read the first line, and so forth. Providing this repetition gives children multiple opportunities to learn the rhyme "by heart" and many children will learn to read the rhyme as well.

CHILDREN'S LITERATURE CITED IN THIS CHAPTER

How Do Dinosaurs Eat Their Food? by Jane Yolen (2005). Scholastic.

IDEAS FOR DISCUSSION, REFLECTION, AND ACTION

1. Name three classroom activities that would enhance the language skills mentioned in this chapter. Write down the dialogue teachers might use to help children engage in each activity and to encourage language.

2. Play is important for many reasons for young children. Several literacy-enriched play settings are discussed in the chapter. Think of another setting and discuss the materials you would place in that area to enhance oral language.

3. Utilize LEA. Select a theme and use the five steps listed in Table 4.1 to carry out this experience with your children.

4. Like the language-friendly classroom, the home environment needs to be language rich as well. Write a newsletter (e-mail, brochure, PowerPoint presentation) for parents and caregivers that explains the importance of making time for conversation, using conversational strategies, and using instructional activities that promote high-quality language experiences in the home. Be sure to include clear, relevant explanations that parent and caregivers will understand.

CHAPTER 5

Developing Children's
Listening Comprehension

Ms. King's preschool classroom of 3- and 4-year-olds is outside playing on the playground when it begins to snow. It is the first snow of the year, and the children are quite excited. Four-year-old Kyle says, "Look, there is a flake on my jacket!" Some children cup their hands to catch the flakes, and others open up their mouths and lean their heads back to let the flakes fall on their tongues. The snow is falling fast in big flakes, and it covers the ground in minutes. Children start to write their names and draw pictures in the snow on the ground. It seems to be getting colder and windy, so Ms. King suggests it is time to go inside. Taking advantage of this event when they return to the classroom, Ms. King picks out the book *The Snowy Day* by Ezra Jack Keats (1976) to read to the children, saying, "Look what I found, it is a book about snow."

The children come to the literacy center to listen to the read-aloud. Ms. King has a Big Book version on an easel so the children can easily see the words and the illustrations. Before reading, Ms. King tells the children that the story is about a little boy named Peter who goes out into the snow and does a lot of things. She asks them to try to remember one or two of the things he does. She also says that every time she says the /sss/ sound, that is their clue to say the word *snow*. Then she will write the word on the experience chart next to her.

The children listen very attentively to remember what things Peter did in the snow, and every time Ms. King looks at them and says the /sss/ sound, they chime in and say the word *snow*.

Ms. King reads, "One winter morning Peter woke up and looked out the window. Ssss . . . [everyone says *snow*] had fallen during the night. It covered everything as far as he could see. After breakfast he put on his

ssss . . . [everyone says *snow*] suit and ran outside. The ssss . . . [everyone says *snow*] was piled up very high along the street to make a path for walking."

When Ms. King and the children finish reading the book, she asks the children what they remember that Peter did in the story. Elena says, "He made angels." Jack says, "He climbed up a mountain of snow." Brad says, "He made a snowman."

Ms. King asks the children what they have done in the snow that Peter did. One child says she goes sledding, another says he has snowball fights, and still another says she likes to make footprints like Peter did. Juan leans over to Ms. King and whispers, "Can I have that book to take home and read?"

Because there was so much interest in snow, Ms. King brings out her collection of books about snow—which includes *Snowballs* by Lois Ehlert (1999), a book of poems by Jack Prelutsky (2006) titled *It's Snowing! It's Snowing! Winter Poems*, and *Owl Moon* by Jane Yolen (1987)— as an introduction to learning about snow.

The term *best practice* is generally used to describe those instructional approaches and techniques that improve children's learning. Best practices, in short, describe instructional approaches and techniques that help children learn well. These practices have acquired evidence over time that if used with fidelity, children are likely to become proficient in listening comprehension. The NELP report (2008), nearly a decade old, was perhaps the most ambitious effort to synthesize this literature in early reading, highlighting key best practices in the field. This chapter describes several best practices specific to developing listening comprehension when using children's literature in the preschool classroom. These strategies play an important role in children's future reading achievement.

SONGS AND RHYMES

Songs are sung and rhymes can be considered little stories for children to chant at different times of a preschool day. For English language learners, in particular, song and rhymes help them to use their new language orally for the first time. The elements of playing with sounds, group recitation, and movement make it easier for English language learners to participate in these language activities. When learning songs and poems, teachers draw attention to the words and their features. The teacher points out words that rhyme or are unusual, and adds gestures to help children to remember the different words and phrases. The teacher helps children to practice coordinating words and actions to remember the song, poem, or word play. Eventually the children can sing without assistance—and begin to enjoy their language use. Song and rhymes are not strangers to the language and literacy curriculum and bring joy into the preschool day. When teachers use these activities intentionally, they develop children's rhyming, alliteration, new vocabulary, oral language, and listening comprehension necessary for conventional reading and writing. The lesson plan in Figure 5.1 shows how singing supports many of these speaking and listening comprehension skills that lay the foundations for reading.

Song: "Old MacDonald Had a Farm"	
Expectations (Head Start Child Development and Early Learning Framework) • Listens to language during songs, stories, or other learning experiences. • Uses different forms of language. • Identifies and discriminates between words in language. • Identifies and discriminates between separate syllables in words.	
Day 1	Introduce the song; link to current theme; use animal props.
	Sing song with enthusiasm and gusto.
	Ask children to tell favorite animal and the sound it makes.
Day 2	Post written copy of the song; recite (say) song verses and point to the print.
	Ask children to say verses with you (echo read, you say one line and they repeat it).
	Invite children to sing the song with you more than once.
Days 3 and 4	Invite children to recite (say) verses with you.
	Associate sound with animal; initial phoneme play with animal name: *a cow says coo-coo-coo-c[k]ei-c[kei]-o*; Farm Animal Sort: Wild/Domestic.
	Sing song; add movement.
Day 5	Sing song with puppets; post song in library area for reciting.

FIGURE 5.1. Lesson plan using the song "Old MacDonald Had a Farm."

Here's what to do over time:

1. Choose a song verse, chant, nursery rhyme, or short poem.
2. Sing, chant, or say the selection with children. Have them repeat phrases to help them learn the piece.
3. Write the words on sentence strips in front of the children. Say each word as you write the phrases and sentences. Then sing, chant, or say each phrase or sentence as the children watch. Invite them to chime in. Place the strip in the pocket chart. When the entire selection is placed in the chart, sing, chant, or say it through in its entirety while pointing to the words.
4. Have the children close their eyes and mix up the sentence strips. After they open their eyes have them help you put the strips back in order.

DIRECTED LISTENING–THINKING ACTIVITY

When children are read to, they need a structure that provides a purpose for reading or listening. The Directed Listening–Thinking Activity (DLTA) is a storybook reading strategy that sets a purpose for reading and listening to help children focus. When teachers frequently model this structure, children internalize it and apply it when they listen to or pretend-read a familiar story on their own (Morrow, 1984, 2014; Stauffer, 1980).

A DLTA can have many different objectives. The framework, however, is always the same: (1) preparation for listening or reading through questions and discussion before reading, (2) reading the story with few interruptions, and (3) discussion after reading. All three steps focus on the DLTA's specific objectives. A DLTA can focus on literal responses such as recalling details and sequencing, and inferential responses such as interpreting characters' feelings, predicting outcomes, and relating the story to another similar text. It can focus on identifying elements of story structure in both narrative and informational text. Children can also be asked to think about the story and give evidence from the text for their answers. Research has demonstrated that a DLTA promotes the use of oral language and increases story comprehension of young listeners (Morrow, 1984, 2014), just as a Directing Reading and Thinking Activity (DRTA) can increase the story comprehension of young readers (Baumann, Seifert-Kessell, & Jones, 1992; Morrow, 2014; Pearson, Roehler, Dole, & Duffy, 1992).

The following DLTA for *The Gingerbread Man* (McCafferty, 2001) focuses on the skill of sequencing events.

Preparation for Listening

It is crucial to build a background for what is going to be read to the children by introducing the story as follows: "Today I'm going to read a story called *The*

Gingerbread Man. Let's look at the pictures and see if you can tell what the story is going to be about." Encourage children to respond as you turn the pages of the book from beginning to end. This activity is sometimes called a *picture walk* (Fountas & Pinnell, 1996). After the children have offered their ideas, say, "This story is about a little gingerbread man who escapes from the oven and all the people in the town try to chase him because they want to eat this delicious cookie. While I'm reading, try to imagine what will happen to the gingerbread man at the end of the story and why you think this. As I read, try to remember who the gingerbread man ran away from first, then second and third."

Ask questions that build additional background knowledge and set a purpose for listening. Relate the questions to real-life experiences or other books whenever possible: "Have you ever tried to chase a friend but he or she got away? How do you catch someone when he or she is running away? Do you have to be fast to catch someone? Do you know another story where someone or something runs away?"

Once children are familiar with this questioning technique, you can ask them to think of their own questions: "Now that I've told you a little about the story, what did you want to find out when I read it to you?"

Reading the Story with Few Interruptions

Be sure to show the children the pictures as you read the book. Stop only once or twice for reactions, comments, or questions. Don't interrupt the story for lots of discussion because discussion should occur after the story is read. Remind children to study the pictures. Model or scaffold responses to guide them in their thinking, keeping in mind the objectives for this particular DLTA. Some discussion questions for *The Gingerbread Man* could include the following: "Can you remember why the gingerbread man was running? Who was trying to catch him?" If the children do not respond, model responses by changing questions to statements: "The gingerbread man was running so fast because everyone wanted to eat him." Children can also be asked to predict what will happen next.

Discussion after Reading

The postreading discussion is guided by the purpose set for listening to the story such as "What happened to the gingerbread man first? Second?" To be sure children have the opportunity to use language, ask them to retell the story to demonstrate their knowledge of sequence. Allow children to use the pictures in the book to help them recall the story sequence. Ask if this could happen in real life? Why or why not?

THE DIALOGIC READING TECHNIQUE

Dialogic reading is a way of reading with children that encourages and supports conversation about the story; with the story as the center of the conversation. For example, in dialogic reading the adult might ask children what they see in a picture, or what they think a character is going to do next (Albright, Delecki, & Hinkle, 2009). This form of engaged, interactive reading is critical to the development of preliteracy and early literacy skills in young children. To have a substantive conversation that extends children's use of language, you need to apply a set of prompts. You can remember these prompts with the acronym CROWD (Bowman, Donovan, & Burns, 2001):

C. *Completion prompts*: Leave a blank at the end of a sentence for children to fill in. For example, "Jack and Jill went up the hill to fetch a pail of _____." This prompt exercises children's sensitivity to the structure of language.

R. *Recall prompts*: These prompts encourage children to remember what happened in the book. For example, you say, "The little red hen wanted to make some bread. Do you remember what happened when she asked for some help?" Use this prompt to help children organize the story and remember its sequence.

O. *Open-ended prompts*: These prompts focus on the pictures in books. You might say, "It's your turn to read the story. What is happening on this page?" When you encourage children to help tell the story, you provide practice in expressive fluency and attention to detail in illustrations.

W. *What, where, when, and why prompts*: These questions also focus on the pictures in books. When you ask, "What's this?" you are teaching children new words. When you ask, "Why do you think the puppy is sad?" you are encouraging them to retrieve words from their own vocabulary store to express their opinions.

D. *Distancing prompts*: These prompts guide children to make connections between the book and their experience. For example, reading *Brown Bear, Brown Bear, What Do You See?* (Martin & Carle, 1996), you ask, "Do you have goldfish at your house? Does your goldfish have a name?" Distancing allows children to practice their conversational and storytelling skills.

SHARED BOOK READING

Shared book reading is similar to the DLTA and is usually carried out in a whole-class setting, although it may be carried out in small groups as well (Holdaway, 1979). During this activity, teachers model fluent reading for children and help them develop listening skills. A shared reading characteristic is to have children participate in the activity by chanting a phrase or reading a word or taking character parts.

Sharing books enhances children's background knowledge, develops their sense of story structure, and familiarizes them with the language of books (Cullinan, 1992; Morrow, 1985, 2014). The language of books differs from oral language and provides a model for speaking. The following sentences from two well-known picture storybooks make this evident:

- "His scales were every shade of blue and green and purple, with sparkling silver scales among them" (*The Rainbow Fish* by Marcus Pfister, 1999).
- "I'm a troll, from a deep dark hole, / My belly's getting thinner, / I need to eat—and goat's a treat—So I'll have you for my dinner" (*The Three Billy Goats Gruff* by P. C. Asbjornsen & J. E. Moe, 1991).

Shared reading often involves reading from a Big Book. The teacher may use a pointer while reading to emphasize the correspondence between spoken and written words and model the tracking of print.

Children's participation in shared reading might include chanting story refrains, reading key words, or stopping at predictable parts and filling in words and phrases. One popular technique is echo reading, where the teacher reads one line and the children repeat it. After the first reading, the Big Book and regular-size versions should be available for children to explore independently.

Shared book readings can be audio recorded and made available in a section of the literacy center for listening. This provides children with a familiar model of fluent reading. They can emulate the teacher's phrasing and intonation as they "whisper read" with the audio recording.

Research tells us that shared book reading provides an opportunity to teach children new words (Cunningham & Zibulsky, 2014; Robbins & Ehri, 1994; Sénéchal, 1997). Even the single reading of a storybook can have an impact on children's vocabulary learning (Sénéchal & Cornell, 1993). Following are two techniques that guide vocabulary instruction in shared reading of a predictable book you may find helpful in your teaching:

Turn and Tell a Word

Before you read, present each word to the children with an accompanying prop, picture, or action. Say the word, then have the children say the word. Tell the meaning of the word (using a child-friendly definition), and then ask children to turn and tell a friend what the word means. During the reading, stop when you encounter each new word. Briefly tell what the word means. Use a gesture or action to add to word meaning. After the reading, review the words and have the children turn and tell a friend what the word means again.

Word Technique

The Word Technique is used after the text is read (Beck, McKeown, & Kucan, 2013). Select two or three new words that are (1) important and useful for children to know; (2) instructionally powerful for making connections to other words and ideas; and (3) knowledge builders in that they expand word meanings, such as multiple meanings, figurative speech, and so on. Use the following steps:

- *Step 1*: Remind children of how the word was used in the story.
- *Step 2*: Ask children to repeat the word to create a sound impression of the word.
- *Step 3*: Explain the meaning of the word in child-friendly language.
- *Step 4*: Provide examples in sentences different from the story.
- *Step 5*: Ask children to provide their own phrases or sentences with your support.
- *Step 6*: Ask children to say the word again to establish phonological awareness of it.
- *Step 7*: End by using all the new words together.

REPEATED READINGS

When a story is read repeatedly, it becomes familiar and comfortable, like singing a well-known song. In addition to offering the pleasure of familiarity, repeated storybook reading helps children to remember new vocabulary and deepens understanding. In a study with 4-year-olds (Morrow, 1987), one group listened to three repeated readings of the same story and the other group listened to three different stories. In an analysis of the discussions that followed the stories, the researchers found that during the course of the study, the responses of the children in the repeated reading group grew in number, variety, and complexity in comparison to the group that had a different story read to them each time. The children in the repeated reading group's responses became more interpretive and they began to predict outcomes and make associations, judgments, and elaborative comments. Children also began to narrate stories as the teacher read and to focus on elements of print, asking names of letters and words. Even children who had limited vocabulary and were not able to comprehend what was read to them made more responses with repeated readings than with a single reading (Morrow, 1987; Pressley & Hilden, 2002).

Repeated readings promote independent reading; children can confidently revisit a familiar book without adult assistance. Children who are able to read independently or participate in pretend-reading behaviors often will select the same book to look at or read it over and over again. Teachers can repeat readings of stories to children in a shared reading setting, encourage children to look at books more than once, and carry out discussions about books that have been pre-viously discussed. Following is an example (from Morrow, 2005, pp. 171–172) of a shared book reading with a 4-year-old. Her responses to a third reading of *The Little Red Hen* (Galdone, 1973) highlight the child's comments and questions and the teacher's responses; most of the story text has been omitted.

> TEACHER: Today I'm going to read a story called *The Little Red Hen*. It is about a hen who wanted some help when she baked some bread. (*Begins to read the story*.) "Who will help me to cut this wheat?"
>
> MELONY: " 'Not I,' said the cat. 'Not I,' said the dog. 'Not I,' said the mouse."
>
> TEACHER: That was good, Melony. You are reading. (*Continues reading*.) "Who will take this wheat to the mill to be ground into flour?"
>
> MELONY: " 'Not I,' said the cat. 'Not I,' said the dog. 'Not I,' said the mouse with the whiskers."
>
> TEACHER: Very nice, Melony. (*Continues to read*.)
>
> MELONY: I want to read that part, but I don't know how.
>
> TEACHER: Go ahead and try. I bet you can. I'll help you: "The cat smelled it."
>
> MELONY: (*Pretend-reads parts she remembers from the repeated readings*.) "The cat smelled it and she said 'Umm that smells good,' and the mouse smelled it, and it smelled good."
>
> TEACHER: (*Continues reading*.) "Who will eat this cake?"
>
> MELONY: "The mouse, the doggy, the kitty!"
>
> TEACHER: You're right again, Melony. (*Reads to the end of the story*.) Did you want to say anything else about the story?
>
> MELONY: He was bad so he couldn't have no cake. (*Searches through the pages*.) That's the wrong part.
>
> TEACHER: Show me the part you are talking about.
>
> MELONY: There it is, almost at the end. She's going to make a cake and she'll say, "Who's going to bake this cake for me?" And the cat says, "Not I," the dog says, "Not I," the mouse says, "Not I." And then when she's cooking it they smell a good thing and then they wanted some, too, but they didn't have any, 'cause they didn't plant the wheat.
>
> TEACHER: That's terrific, Melony.

The kinds of sophisticated responses found in this example are more likely to occur when a child has heard the same story many times.

Predictable stories are ideal for shared reading experiences because they invite children to guess what will happen next. Predictability takes many forms. The use of catchphrases, such as "A house is a house for me" in the story *A House Is a*

House for Me (Hoberman, 2007), encourages children to read along. Predictable rhyme, as in *Goodnight Moon* (Brown, 2007), makes it easy for children to fill in words. Cumulative patterns contribute to predictability. New events are added with each episode, then repeated in the next, as in *Are You My Mother?* (Eastman, 1998). This book repeats phrases and episode patterns as its central character, a baby bird, searches for his mother by approaching different animals and asking the same question: "Are you my mother?" Look for books that highlight familiar sequences, such as days of the week, months of the year, letters, and numbers, such as *The Very Hungry Caterpillar* (Carle, 1994). Conversation can also contribute to predictability, as in *The Three Billy Goats Gruff* (Asbjornsen & Moe, 1991) or *The Three Little Pigs* (Galdone, 1984).

Predictable books are excellent for young children who are just beginning to experiment with *emergent literacy* practices, as well as for conventional readers. They allow the child's first experience with reading to be enjoyable and successful with minimal effort. Such immediate success encourages the child to continue efforts at reading. For example, after one 4-year-old had listened to *The Little Engine That Could* (Piper, 1978), which has a repeated phrase throughout, she said, "Show me where it says, 'I think I can, I think I can.' I want to see it in the book." When the teacher showed her the text, the child repeated each word while pointing to it and then asked to see the words in another part of the book. She proceeded to search through the rest of the book, reading with great enthusiasm each time she found the line, "I think I can, I think I can." This was an enjoyable success experience in this child's beginning efforts at reading.

SMALL-GROUP AND ONE-TO-ONE STORYBOOK READING

Small-group and one-to-one readings are effective in the preschool classroom because it is easier for preschoolers to pay attention to the teacher in settings with small numbers of children. One of the greatest benefits of one-to-one story reading is the interaction that results. Children gain a great deal of information from this close interaction, while adults discover what children know and what they want to learn.

It has been found that one-to-one readings are especially beneficial for preschoolers who have had little experience with books at home (Morrow, 1988b). When reading in small groups or in a one-to-one setting, it is important for teachers to encourage children to be interactive by asking them to respond to questions, discuss pictures in the book, and chant repeated phrases.

When teachers read to children frequently and initiate interactive discussions, the number and complexity of the children's responses increase. Children offer many questions and comments that focus on meaning. Initially, they label illustrations; eventually they give more attention to details. Their comments and questions become interpretive and predictive and they draw from their own experiences.

They also begin narrating—that is "reading" or mouthing the story along with the teacher.

When involved in frequent small-group or one-to-one storybook readings, children begin to focus on structural elements in a story, remarking on titles, settings, characters, and story events. After many readings, the children begin to focus on print, matching sounds and letters, and reading words (Morrow, 1987). When children hear stories in small groups, they tend to respond more; they repeat one another's remarks and elaborate on what their peers have said. Figure 5.2 provides guidelines for teacher interactive behavior during small-group and one-to-one story readings.

Productive discussions result from good questions. Good questions ask children to clarify information and predict outcomes. The major types of question-and-answer relationships can be summarized as follows:

Literal questions ask students to . . .

- Identify details such as who, what, when, and where.
- Classify ideas.
- Sequence text.
- Find the main idea.

Teacher role	Teaching actions (guidance)
Manage	Introduce story.
	Provide background information about the book.
	Redirect irrelevant discussion back to the story.
Prompt responses	Prompt children to ask questions or comment throughout the story when there are natural places to stop.
	Model responses for children if they are not responding (e.g., "Those animals aren't very nice. They won't help the little red hen").
	Relate responses to real-life experiences (e.g., "I needed help when I was preparing a party, and my family shared the work. Did you ever ask for help and not get it? What happened?").
	When children do not respond, ask questions that require answers other than *yes* or *no* (e.g., "What would you have done if you were the little red hen and no one helped you bake the bread?").
Support and inform	Answer questions as they are asked.
	React to comments.
	Relate your responses to real-life experiences.
	Provide positive reinforcement for children's responses.

FIGURE 5.2. Teacher interactive behavior to encourage discussion and comprehension during small-group and one-to-one storybook reading. From Morrow (1988b). Copyright 1988 by the International Reading Association. Reprinted by permission.

Inferential and critical questions ask students to . . .

- Draw information from their background knowledge.
- Relate text to life experiences.
- Relate text to text experiences.
- Predict outcomes ("What do you think will happen next?").
- Interpret text ("Put yourself in the place of the characters; what would you do?").
- Compare and contrast.
- Determine cause and effect.
- Apply information.
- Solve problems.

Discussion questions should reflect children's interests and have many appropriate responses rather than just one correct answer. Questions with one correct answer can be asked occasionally, but the majority of questions should stimulate discussion and invite children to share their thoughts and feelings about the text. Include a few questions that deal with facts, main ideas, and story details. When asking questions, have children refer to the illustrations for possible answers. Once children are experienced at responding to questions, they can be encouraged to ask their own questions about a story that was read to them.

The following examples of small-group storybook reading illustrate the kinds of questions children ask and responses they make when they are engrossed in the reading experience. The examples reveal the rich information children receive from the adult reader and indicate what the children already know and what their interests are—useful information for anyone designing instruction.

Example 1

Story: *A Splendid Friend Indeed* (Bloom, 2006)—The child asks questions about book concepts.

> MADELINE: (Points to the illustration on the book cover.) Why does it have a picture on it?
>
> TEACHER: The cover of the book has a picture on it so you will know what the story is about. Look at the picture. Can you tell what the book might be about?
>
> JEANNINE: Ummm, I think it is about a big white furry bear and a duck and they like each other because they are smiling at each other.
>
> TEACHER: You're right, very good. The book is about a polar bear and a duck and they are good friends. The title of the book is *A Splendid Friend Indeed*. The pictures on the cover of a book and inside the book can help you figure out what the words say.

Example 2

Story: *A Splendid Friend Indeed* (Bloom, 2006)—The child asks for a definition.

> TEACHER: I'm going to read the story *A Splendid Friend Indeed*.
>
> JEANNINE: What is splendid?
>
> TEACHER: Splendid means wonderful, very good, terrific. Do you have a splendid friend?
>
> JEANNINE: Devin is my best friend. I guess she is splendid. I will tell her.

Example 3

Story: *Are You My Mother?* (Eastman, 1998)—The child attends to print.

> JORDON: Wait, stop reading. Let me see this again. (He looks at the page.) That says, "Are you my mother?"
>
> TEACHER: You're right. Can you find it anywhere else?
>
> JORDON: I think so. Yes, here it is on this page. "Are you my mother?" And again over   here, "Are you my mother?"
>
> TEACHER: That is great, you are reading.

Example 4

Story: *The Mitten* (Tresselt, 1989)—The child predicts.

> CHARLENE: I wonder if that mitten is going to break open?
>
> TEACHER: Why do you think that?
>
> CHARLENE: Well, it is a mitten for a little boy so it isn't so big. All of those animals are going in it. Soon they won't fit.
>
> TEACHER: Those are good ideas, Charlene. I'll read on and we will find out if you are right.

Example 5

Story: *Knuffle Bunny* (Willems, 2004)—The child makes connections from one text to another.

> JUAN: Hey, this book is like the Mary Poppins DVD.
>
> TEACHER: What do you mean?
>
> JUAN: Well, you see the pictures in *Knuffle Bunny* in the back are real like

real buildings and parks and stuff someone took those pictures with a camera of real things, and the pictures in the front are cartoons somebody drawed. In the Mary Poppins DVD there are real people and then sometimes there are cartoon people and cartoon pictures, too.

Example 6

Story: *Madeline's Rescue* (Bemelmans, 1953)—The child relates the text to real-life experience.

ABRIEL: What's the policeman going to do?

TEACHER: He's going to help Madeline. Policemen are nice; they always help us.

ABRIEL: Policemans aren't nice. See, my daddy beat up Dominic and the policeman came and took him away and put him in jail. And my Daddy cried and I cried. I don't like policemans. I don't think they are nice.

These examples reveal children's understanding of text. The children's comments and questions not only relate to literal meanings but also raise interpretive and critical issues by associating the story with their own lives, making predictions about what will happen next in a story, or expressing judgments about characters' actions. Their responses also relate to matters of print, such as names of letters, words, and sounds.

Although whole-class readings are practical and effective in exposing children to literature, they do not promote the interaction between adults and children that takes place in small-group and one-to-one readings. If we review transcripts of story readings in all three settings, several things become apparent. In whole-class settings, children are discouraged from asking questions or commenting during the story because doing so interrupts the flow of the story for the rest of the audience. In this setting, the discussion has to be managed by the teacher to such an extent that he or she often talks more than the children do. Because of the size of the group, a truly interactive situation cannot exist. However, in small-group and one-to-one story readings, a teacher may manage and prompt the discussion at first, but only to encourage and model responses for children (the coding form in Figure 5.3 can be used during these readings). The roles reverse in a short time, and soon most of the dialogue is initiated by the children (Morrow, 1987).

Children who do not experience one-to-one readings at home are at a disadvantage in their literacy development. By reading to a child individually in the classroom, the teacher can compensate for what is not provided at home. With frequent one-to-one reading, children gain both literacy skills and positive attitudes toward books; they learn to associate books with warmth and pleasure. Time limitations and class size make it difficult to provide small-group and one-to-one

Directions: Read a story to one child or a small group of children. Encourage the children to respond with questions and comments. Record the session. Transcribe or listen to the recording, noting each child's responses by placing checks in the appropriate categories. A category may receive more than one check, and a single response may be credited to more than one category. Total the number of checks in each category.

Child's Name: _____ Date: _____

Name of Story: _____

1. Focus on Story Structure
_____ identifies setting (time, place)
_____ identifies characters
_____ identifies theme (problem or goal)
_____ recalls plot episodes (events leading toward problem solution or goal attainment)
_____ identifies resolution

2. Focus on Meaning
_____ labels pictures
_____ identifies details
_____ interprets characters and events (makes associations, elaborations)
_____ predicts events
_____ draws from personal experience
_____ seeks definitions of words
_____ uses narration behavior (recites parts of the book along with the teacher)

3. Focus on Print
_____ asks questions or makes comments about letters
_____ asks questions or makes comments about sounds
_____ asks questions or makes comments about words
_____ reads words
_____ reads sentences

4. Focus on Illustrations
_____ asks questions or makes comments about illustrations

FIGURE 5.3. Coding children's responses during story readings. From Morrow (1988b). Copyright 1988 by the International Reading Association. Reprinted by permission.

readings in school, but asking aides, volunteers, and older children to help can alleviate these problems.

STORYTELLING

Storytelling is an old, time-honored activity used by all cultures to teach children about their immediate environment and the wider world. Most cultures engage in storytelling, so it is familiar to children from many different backgrounds. It is also one of the earliest expressions of the language arts to appear in children. Every child has a story to tell and seeks an audience for it, even if the audience is composed of stuffed animals and dolls.

As a best practice, storytelling is a valuable medium for developing the oral language skills and active listening to comprehend. To understand a storyteller, children need to be active listeners—predicting, checking, and integrating what they hear into a comprehensible story. To be storytellers, they must use their expressive vocabulary, narrative skills, and sense of audience to tell a good story.

When you implement this best practice, bring storytellers from different cultures to the classroom. Have stories told in the home languages of your English language learners; they will provide those children with a sense of pride in their home languages and will provide the English-speaking children with the understanding that storytelling is a part of many cultural traditions.

Becoming Storytellers

The instructional framework of storytelling is a three-part structure that (1) models storytelling for children, (2) guides the development of storytelling skills, and (3) supports children as storytellers. This model–guide–support framework can be implemented over the entire program year as an integral part of your language and literacy program.

Storytelling on your part begins with the selection of several good stories to tell over time. You will use these storytelling events as a way to model storytelling skills for your children. Some helpful guidelines (Breneman & Breneman, 1983) for selecting stories are as follows:

- The story is age-level appropriate with easily understood words.
- The plot has action and creates a stage for what is to come.
- The story uses repetition, rhyming phrases, or silly words.
- The values and models presented are appropriate for today's children.
- The characters are memorable.
- Taste, smell, sight, sound, and tactile descriptions create richness and depth.
- The story line is strong, clear, and logical.
- The storyteller likes the story and is eager to share it.

When modeling good storytelling as a guide for children know the story thoroughly in your mind. Consider using props, such as felt-board figures, puppets, music, objects, pictures, on-the-spot sketches, and technology. Emphasize repetitive phrases so children can join in. Vary your tone, speed, volume, and pitch to pique and sustain interest. And, of course, rehearse the story several times before orally telling it.

Once you have modeled a few good stories, help children start to tell their own stories and begin to build up their storytelling skills. At first, you may need to provide them with storytelling ideas and topics, such as a retelling of a well-known fairytale or relating a personal experience. Show them a few basic storytelling strategies, such as using props, varying your voice, and rehearsing the story out loud. Confer with your new storytellers to prepare a storytelling session. The storyteller should connect with the story listener. Conducted regularly and in a sensitive, supportive manner, storytelling exercises a full complement of oral language skills, including the following:

- Demonstrating language cohesion (logical, sequenced).
- Using tone, volume, pace, intonation, and gesture to enhance meaning.
- Taking into account audience and purpose when speaking.
- Using vocabulary.
- Practicing models of correct English.

Learning How to Be a Storyteller

Because storytelling skills encompass so many dimensions of oral language, they are developed gradually. Storytelling abilities are built from strong, clear models. Storytellers should be well prepared as a result of practicing. Use appropriate expression for the theme of the story. Encourage participation by students with repeated phrases. The preschooler audience gets a chance to practice their best listening comprehension skills.

Include storytelling as a regular activity in your themes and units. Ultimately we want children not only to become storytellers but to create their own stories and tell them as well.

STORY RETELLING

Story retelling is different from storytelling. When children retell stories they have listened to or read, their vocabulary, syntax, comprehension, and sense of story structure are mutually developed (Cunningham & Zibulsky, 2014; Ritchie et al., 2002). Retelling allows for original thinking as children incorporate their own life experiences into their retelling (Gambrell, Pfeiffer, & Wilson, 1985). With practice in retelling, children assimilate the concept of narrative or expository text structure. They learn to introduce a narrative story with its beginning and its setting, theme, plot episodes, and resolution. Children learn to distinguish the main ideas from the supporting details. They also interpret the sounds and expressions of characters' voices. In retelling expository text, children learn the structures in this type of literature by focusing on sequence of events, cause and effect, or problem and solution. Retelling is not an easy task for children, but with practice they improve quickly. Be sure to inform children before they listen to a story that they will be asked to retell it (Morrow, 1996). Further instructions depend on the purpose of the retelling. If the intent is to teach sequence, for instance, then children should be asked to think about what happened first, second, and so on. If the goal is to teach children to make inferences from the text, ask them to think of personal experiences that are similar to those that happened in the story. Pre- and postdiscussion of text helps to improve retelling ability, as does the teacher's modeling a retelling for children.

Retelling also allows adults to evaluate children's progress. When assessing a retelling, do not offer prompts beyond general ones such as "What happened next?" or "Can you think of anything else?" Retellings of narrative text reveal a child's sense of story structure, focusing mostly on literal recall, but they also reflect a child's inferential thinking. To assess the child's retelling for sense of story structure, first divide the events of the story into four categories: setting, theme, plot episodes, and resolution. Refer to the guidelines for story retelling (see Figure 5.4), and use an outline of the text to record the number of ideas and details the child includes within each category in the retelling, regardless of their order. Credit the child for partial recall or for recounting the "gist" of an event (Pellegrini & Galda, 1982). Evaluate the child's sequencing ability by comparing the order of events in the child's retelling with the proper order of setting, theme, plot episodes, and resolution. The analysis indicates not only which elements the child includes or omits and how well the child sequences, but also where instruction might be focused. Comparing analyses of several retellings over a year will indicate the child's progress.

Outlining a story to reveal its structure, characters, and themes creates a framework for evaluating a child's retelling. The outline of *Franklin in the Dark* (Bourgeois, 1986), shown in Figure 5.5, is a typical example of a story outline (Morrow, 1996).

Transcribing a verbatim transcript of a child's story retelling provides teachers with data needed for analysis. Following is a retelling by a 4-year-old of the story *Franklin in the Dark*:

TEACHER: What's the title of the story I read to you today?

PHILIP: I don't know.

Teacher role	Example
Ask the child to retell the story	"A little while ago, I read the story [name of story]. Would you tell the story as if you were telling it to a friend who has never heard it before?"
Use prompts only if needed.	If the child has difficulty beginning the retelling, suggest beginning with "Once upon a time . . ." or "Once there was . . ."
	If the child stops retelling before the end of the story, encourage continuation by asking, "What comes next?" or "Then what happened?"
	If the child stops retelling and cannot continue with general prompts, ask a question that is relevant at the point in the story at which the child has paused—for example, "What was Jenny's problem in the story?"
When a child is unable to retell the story, or if the retelling lacks sequence and detail, prompt the retelling step by step.	"Once upon a time . . ." or "Once there was . . ."
	"Who was the story about?"
	"When did the story happen? Day or night? Summer or winter?"
	"Where did the story happen?"
	"What was the main character's problem in the story?"
	"How did he or she try to solve the problem? What did he or she do first? Second? Next?"
	"How was the problem solved?"
	"How did the story end?"

FIGURE 5.4. Guidelines for story retelling. From Morrow (1988a). Copyright by the author. Reprinted by permission.

Setting	1. Once upon a time there was a turtle named Franklin. 2. Characters: Franklin's mother, a bird, a duck, a lion, and a polar bear.
Theme	Franklin is afraid to go into his shell because it is dark inside his shell.
Plot episodes	*First episode:* Franklin decides to look for help to solve his problem.
	Second episode: Franklin meets a duck and asks for help. The duck tells Franklin that he wears water wings because he is afraid of the water.
	Third episode: Franklin meets a lion who wears ear muffs because he is afraid of his own roar.
	Fourth episode: Franklin meets a bird who uses a parachute because he is afraid to fly.
	Fifth episode: Franklin meets a polar bear who wears a hat, mittens, and a scarf because he doesn't like the cold.
	Sixth episode: Franklin shares his experiences with his mother.
Resolution	1. Franklin and his mother put a night-light in his shell. 2. Franklin is no longer afraid to go into his shell.

FIGURE 5.5. *Franklin in the Dark* story outline.

TEACHER: *Franklin in the Dark.*

PHILIP: *Franklin in the Dark.* One time Franklin didn't want to go in his shell. He was too scared. But his Mama says there's nothing in there. But Franklin didn't want to go in the shell because he thought there was monsters in there. He didn't like to go in because he was scared. It was dark. At the end he went in, he turned on a little night-light and went to sleep. That's it.

Retellings can be evaluated for many different comprehension tasks. The directions to students prior to retelling and the method of analysis should match the goal. Figure 5.6 provides an analysis form for evaluating a retelling. The teacher checks for elements that a child includes and determines progress over time.

Setting

_____ Begins the story with an introduction.

_____ Names the main character.

_____ Lists the other characters.

_____ Includes a statement about time and place.

Theme

_____ Refers to the main character's primary goal or problem to be solved.

Plot episodes

_____ Recalls episodes.

_____ Lists episodes recalled.

Resolution

_____ Includes the solution to the problem or the attainment of the goal.

_____ Includes an ending to the story.

Sequence

_____ Tells the story in a sequential order.

FIGURE 5.6. Analysis of story retelling.

In his retelling, Philip names the main characters: Franklin and Franklin's mother. Philip restates the problem, the main character, and the theme. He understands the resolution of the story, and his retelling has a clear ending. The parts of the story that Philip included are told in sequential order. However, Philip's retelling does not begin with an introduction. There is no statement of time and place. Aside from mentioning Franklin and his mother, Philip does not talk about any of the other four characters, nor does he recall any of the episodes in the story. From this evaluation, it is evident that Philip is able to recall the theme of the story, the resolution; future instruction should focus on recalling story details such as characters and plot episodes and beginning retellings with an introduction.

To illustrate progress over time, the following is a sample of a retelling of *Jenny Learns a Lesson* (Fujikawa, 1980) by Philip at the end of the school year, 8 months after the first retelling (the first part of this example is an outline of the story, and the second part of the example is the student's retelling).

Story Outline

1. Once upon a time there was a girl who liked to play pretend.
2. *Characters:* Jenny (main character), Nicholas, Sam, Mei Su, and Shags, the dog.
3. *Theme:* Every time Jenny played with her friends, she bossed them.
4. *Plot episodes*
   - First episode: Jenny decided to pretend to be a queen. She called her friends. They came to play. Jenny told them all what to do and was bossy. The friends became angry and left.
   - Second episode: Jenny decided to play dancer. She called her friends and they came to play. Jenny told them all what to do. The friends became angry and left.
   - Third episode: Jenny decided to play pirate. She called her friends and they came to play. Jenny told them all what to do. The friends became angry and left.
   - Fourth episode: Jenny decided to play duchess. She called her friends and they came to play. Jenny told them all what to do. The friends became angry and left.
   - Fifth episode: Jenny's friends refused to play with her because she was so bossy. Jenny became lonely and apologized to them for being bossy.
5. *Resolution:* The friends all played together, and each person did what he or she wanted to do. They all had a wonderful day and were so tired that they fell asleep.

Student's Retelling

"Once upon a time there's a girl named Jenny and she called her friends over and they played queen and went to the palace. They had to, they had to do what she said and they didn't like it so then they went home and said that was boring. It's not fun playing queen and doing what she says you have to. So they didn't play with her for 7 days and she had an idea that she was being selfish, so she went to find her friends and said, 'I'm sorry I was so mean.' And said, 'Let's play pirate,' and they played pirate and they went onto the ropes. Then they played that she was a fancy lady playing house. And they have tea. And they played what they wanted and they were happy. The end."

In this retelling of the story, Philip includes more characters, details, and episodes than he did in his first retelling, illustrating his progress in developing comprehension skills.

GRAPHIC ORGANIZERS

Graphic organizers are visual illustrations or representations of text information that help readers see relationships between concepts or events in a narrative or expository writing. They can help teach many elements needed for comprehension, such as vocabulary, cause and effect, problem solving, and so on. Following are some well-known types of graphic organizers. We have also used well-known books to demonstrate, which should help the reader understand the concepts.

Webs

Webs are graphic representations, or diagrams, for categorizing and structuring information. They help children see how words and ideas are related to one another. Webs tend to be drawn using a spiderlike effect. Webbing strategies build on children's prior knowledge. They help the child retrieve what is known about a topic and use the information in reading and listening to text. Research has demonstrated that the use of webbing develops vocabulary and comprehension.

K-W-L

K-W-L is a cognitive strategy to enhance comprehension. It is used mainly with expository text and can be adapted for use with narrative stories. K-W-L stands for What We *Know*, What We *Want* to Know, and What We *Learned* (Ogle, 1986). With this technique students use prior knowledge to create interest about what is to be read to them. It helps set a purpose for listening to direct thinking, and it encourages sharing of ideas. The following are the steps involved in putting the strategy into practice.

1. Before reading expository text, children brainstorm what they think they know about a topic. For example, if the book they are going to read is *Volcanoes* (Branley, 2008), the class would list What We *Know* about volcanoes.
2. Children list questions about What We *Want* to Know about volcanoes before reading the book.
3. After reading the text, children make a list of What We *Learned* about volcanoes.

After reading the book, children can compare information learned from the text with what they already knew before reading the book. They can determine what they learned as a result of reading the text and, finally, what is still on the list of what they would like to learn because it was not included in the book.

Venn Diagrams

A *Venn diagram* is a graphic organizer that uses two overlapping circles to show relationships between ideas. The Venn diagram helps to compare two or three concepts in a text (Nagy, 1988). When comparing two concepts, we list the main characteristics of each in the outer circles and the characteristics in common in the intersection. The Venn diagram can be used with expository or narrative text.

CONCLUSION

It is clear that there are many ways to enhance listening comprehension with young children. Some of the ideas presented in this chapter are those that many teachers do already. It is important to recognize what skills are being taught. We sing and tell stories with young children, however, when done with the idea that these activities can enhance comprehension makes them more intentional. When we share literature it should be with a purpose in mind so that we systematically teach comprehension skills. We know that we need to read stories in a dialogic manner with discussion before reading to set a purpose and discussion after the reading to encourage critical thinking. We know it is important to repeat stories read, and not only read to the whole class but small groups as well. Storytelling is important since it is a tradition in so many cultures. Immerse your students in literacy and purposely build listening with interactive discussions. The children will grow to enjoy literature and learn how to comprehend.

Following are three ideas from preschool classroom teachers. They are all using graphic organizers with their children to help with comprehending stories they read to them. One uses a web, one uses a K-W-L chart, and the other a Venn diagram. They write words on the charts, but not many. They all include illustrations.

Web

Ms. Fife used a webbing activity to help with vocabulary concepts in the story she read to the children—for example, after reading *The Snowy Day* (Keats, 1976) she made a circle in the middle of a chart and wrote the word *snow* in the middle of the circle. She asked the children to brainstorm ideas about what snow was like. Jennifer said, "Snow is cold." Ms. Fife drew a line out from the circle and at the end of the line wrote *cold*. Other children said, "Snow is white, mushy, and slippery." Ms. Fife made three more lines to put these words on. Next she asked the children, "What things can you do in the snow?" Ms. Fife added lines and wrote the words the children generated as well as an illustration such as make angels, go sledding, make snowballs, and snowmen. A sample of that web is shown in Figure 5.7.

K-W-L

In the following vignette we see Ms. Bell using the K-W-L graphic organizer to teach informational text.

Ms. Bell was going to read a story about fruit. Before reading the expository text, children were asked to brainstorm what they know about fruit. Then she did a

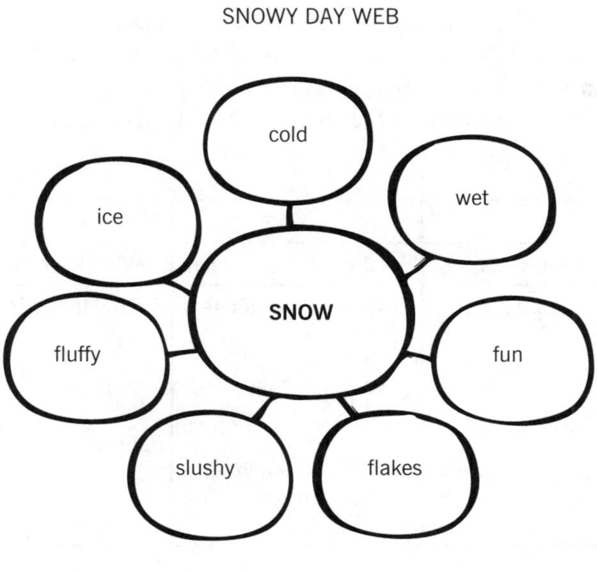

SNOWY DAY WEB

FIGURE 5.7. Example of a word web about snow.

K-W-L chart with the children and asked, "What do you know about fruit?" Children named kinds of fruit, such as apples, oranges, peaches, pears, bananas, and plums. She wrote that in the K section of the chart and drew them as well. She then asked the children, "What would you like to know about fruit?" and the children said, "How do they grow? Where do they grow? Why are they good for you?" She wrote those in the W section of the K-W-L chart. After she read the story, she asked "What did you learn?" Josh said, "Fruit grows mostly in the summer and fall." One child said that most fruit grows on trees. Another child said they have lots of good vitamins in them so they are good for us. The teacher wrote this in the L part of the chart (see Figure 5.8).

Venn Diagrams

Preschoolers can work with Venn diagrams to see likenesses and differences between texts. It would also allow them to make text connections. Ms. Taylor read *The Three Little Pigs* (Galdone, 1984) and, on another day, *Goldie Locks and the Three Bears* (Daley & Russell, 1999). After hearing *Goldie Locks*, Ms. Taylor flashed a Venn diagram on a smartboard and said to the children, "Remember we read *The Three Little Pigs*, and today we read *Goldilocks and the Three Bears*? What is the same about both of these books?" Peter said, "They each have three of the same animals." Justin added, "They each have only four characters in each story, and they both take place in homes." After that Ms. Taylor asked, "How are the stories different?" Ashley said *Goldie Locks* has bears and a girl and *The Three Pigs* has pigs and a wolf. Max said, "Nothing got broken in *The Three Pigs*, and in *Goldilocks* a lot got broken." This is a comprehension strategy used throughout the grades. Note the Venn diagram for these stories in Figure 5.9.

CHILDREN'S LITERATURE CITED IN THIS CHAPTER

Are You My Mother? by P. D. Eastman (1998). Random House.
Brown Bear, Brown Bear, What Do You See? by Eric Carle (1967). Holt.
Franklin in the Dark by Paulette Bourgeois (1986). Scholastic.
The Gingerbread Man by Catherine McCafferty (2001). Houghton Mifflin.

K	W	L
What we KNOW	What we WANT to learn	What we LEARNED
There are apples pears peaches plums. Fruit is sweet.	1. What do the different fruit trees look like? 2. Where do fruits grow? 3. When do you know a fruit is ready to eat?	1. Fruit grows in the summer and fall. 2. Fruit grows on trees. 3. Fruits have vitamins.

FIGURE 5.8. Example of a K-W-L chart about fruit.

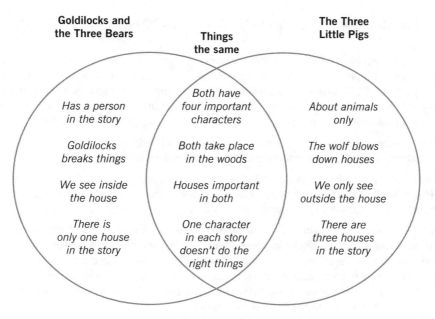

**Goldilocks and
the Three Bears**

**Things
the same**

**The Three
Little Pigs**

*Has a person
in the story*

*Both have
four important
characters*

*About animals
only*

*Goldilocks
breaks things*

*Both take place
in the woods*

*The wolf blows
down houses*

*We see inside
the house*

*Houses important
in both*

*We only see
outside the house*

*There is
only one house
in the story*

*One character
in each story
doesn't do the
right things*

*There are
three houses
in the story*

FIGURE 5.9. Example of a Venn diagram.

Goldie Locks and the Three Bears by Audrey Daly and Chris Russell (1999). Ladybird
Books.
Goodnight Moon by Margaret Wise Brown (2007). HarperCollins.
A House Is a House for Me by Mary Ann Hoberman (2007). Puffin Books.
It's Snowing! It's Snowing! Winter Poems by Jack Prelutsky (2006). HarperCollins.
Jenny Learns a Lesson by Gyo Fujikawa (1980). Grosset and Dunlap.
Knuffle Bunny by Mo Willems (2004). Hyperion Books.
The Little Engine That Could by Watty Piper (1978). Grosset and Dunlap.
The Little Red Hen by Paul Galdone (1985). Grosset and Dunlap.
Madeline's Rescue by Ludwig Bemelmans (1953). Viking Books.
The Mitten by Alvin Tresselt (1989). HarperCollins.
Owl Moon by Jane Yolen (1987). Philomel Books.
The Rainbow Fish by Marcus Pfister (1999). North-South Books.
Snowballs by Lois Ehlert (1999). Houghton Mifflin Harcourt.
The Snowy Day by Ezra Jack Keats (1976). Puffin Books.
A Splendid Friend Indeed by Suzanne Bloom (2006). Scholastic.
The Three Billy Goats Gruff by P. C. Asbjornsen and J. E. Moe (1991). Houghton Mifflin
Harcourt.
The Three Little Pigs (Galdone, 1984). Houghton Mifflin Harcourt.
The Very Hungry Caterpillar by Eric Carle (2007). Penguin Group.
Volcanoes by Franklyn M. Branley (2008). HarperCollins.

IDEAS FOR DISCUSSION, REFLECTION, AND ACTION

1. This chapter includes strategies to help children comprehend stories. Working together with colleagues, have different teachers select different strategies, such as story retelling, reading a story using a DLTA format, repeat readings, and reading to small groups. Each teacher can carry out the strategy with his or her children and reflect upon how the children responded and improved their comprehension.

2. In this chapter, four types of storybook reading are described: shared book reading, the DLTA, and dialogic reading. How are these the same, and how are they different?

3. To practice becoming a storyteller, select a story you like and learn it but don't memorize it. Practice telling the story while you look at yourself in the mirror and, when you are comfortable, videotape yourself telling the story. Evaluate your presentation.

4. Story retelling is an excellent way to enhance and assess comprehension. Select two books with illustrations that are similar in genre, numbers of pages, number of words, and number of different words. Parse each story as described in this chapter. Have a child retell one story, and then score the story based on the description in this chapter. Work on these skills with the child over a period of about 4 weeks. Then read the second book to the child and score the retelling. In what areas has the child improved?

CHAPTER 6

Reading with Children at Home

Mrs. Jones spreads the newspaper on the table as her 5-year-old grandson sits next to her. She takes out the sports section since they had just seen a college football game that was written about in the local paper.

DARREN: What was the score again? I forget.

MRS. JONES: Let's look together and figure it out. Can you read those numbers?

DARREN: That's Rutgers, 13, and Syracuse, 7.

MRS. JONES: Very good.

DARREN: Who is that player in the picture?

> MRS. JONES: (*Gets out the book they bought at the game and looks to see who number 23 was. When they find out, Mrs. Jones reads about him to Darren.*)
>
> DARREN: How far is Syracuse? Can we go there?
>
> MRS. JONES: It is about a 4-hour drive to get there. (*Gets out a map and shows Darren where he lives in New Jersey and where Syracuse is in New York.*)

In the preceding vignette—a conversation between a boy and his grandmother—the discussion made use of new vocabulary, reading, math, and geography. The newspaper was the form of literature that served as the basis of the discussion.

As illustrated in this vignette, children's first and most enduring teachers are the family members who care for them. The success of any preschool literacy program largely depends on the literacy environment at home. Schools must involve parents as an integral part of their literacy programs. Because families come in many forms, we use the term *parent* to refer to any adult who is responsible for the child's care at home.

WHY IS FAMILY LITERACY IMPORTANT?

We can attest to the vital role of the home in the development of early literacy. From the day our children were born, they were read to. They were read to by their parents and grandparents. Every day, they snuggled up for story time, always in the same chair, sitting in the reader's lap. By 5 months, these children could listen as they were read to. Many books were read to these children. There were board books with short stories and only a few words on each page, such as *The Very Hungry Caterpillar* (Carle, 1994). As we read to these children, they began to focus intently on the brightly colored pictures. The children would smile or be serious, but they were engaged. They reached out to touch the books. Occasionally they made cooing sounds that seemed like attempts to imitate the reading voice. Through this daily experience, they became familiar with storybook reading and welcomed them.

As months went by, the children responded to books in new ways. By 10 months, they began to turn the pages of the book. By 12 months, they pointed to pictures and made sounds as if naming objects or characters. The family responded with pleasure; this attention and encouragement motivated the babies to keep exploring books. We talked about the words and pictures, expanding story concepts. Storybook reading was a pleasant and relaxing ritual that everyone looked forward to.

By the time these children were 15 months old, they could be found sitting on the floor "reading" a book. They knew how to hold the book right-side up, they knew where the beginning of the book was and the end, and they knew how to turn the pages. They looked at the pictures and chanted in tones similar to the sound of the reading. The language was not understandable, but from a distance one might think that these children were reading. Actually they were—not in the conventional manner, but by demonstrating early literacy behavior.

These children had accessible shelves of books. Books were mixed in with toys, and the children were free to use them at all times. These children saw their parents reading, and at times they joined them with one of their books. Their knowledge about books and reading did not just happen. Rather, it developed within an environment that fostered literacy through the guidance, modeling, and encouragement of supportive adults.

PROMOTING ORAL LANGUAGE AND COMPREHENSION IN THE HOME

Children's family members frequently ask teachers what they can do at home to help their children learn to read and write. When families provide a rich literacy environment at home, teaching reading and writing becomes easier for both the teacher and the child at school. Schools need to take responsibility for sharing information in the community about activities that families can implement at home before their children enter preschool. For example, family workshops can be held for parents of children who are not yet of school age, and schools can distribute booklets about literacy development at home from birth to age 3.

The following factors affect the quality of the literacy environment in the home (Leichter, 1984):

- Interpersonal interactions—the literacy experiences shared by children, parents, siblings, and other individuals in the home.
- Physical environment—literacy materials in the home.
- Emotional and motivational climate—family attitudes and aspirations for literacy achievement.

This means that books, magazines, and newspapers are read and discussed among family members. Children have access to many types of reading and writing materials and are encouraged to use them in their daily lives. Parents let children know that they value reading and writing.

In the following sections, we suggest materials and strategies for reading with children at home that preschool teachers can share with families. Because early exposure to print is critical for successful literacy development, we discuss reading with children from birth onward. Parents must be made aware of the work they need to do at home with books before children enter preschool.

MATERIALS TO READ IN THE HOME

Children's books should be made available throughout the home—in the kitchen, the bathroom, and the playroom. Setting up a library corner in each child's bedroom provides children with easy access to books and helps make reading an integral part of a family's daily routine. If a bookshelf is not available, books can be stored in a cardboard box or plastic crate. Before babies are crawling or walking, books can be brought to them in cribs and playpens; waterproof books are perfect for bathtubs.

A well-stocked home library contains many types of books. A more complete list of appropriate books for young children can be found in Appendix A. For babies up to 18 months, brightly colored concept books with cardboard, plastic, or cloth pages are ideal. They must be safe, with rounded edges, and sturdy enough to withstand chewing and other rough treatment. As the child enters the preschool years and beyond, nursery rhymes, fairytales, folktales, realistic literature, informational books, picture books, alphabet books, number books, poetry, books related to favorite television programs, and easy-to-read books (i.e., those with limited vocabularies, large print, and pictures closely associated with the text) should be made available. Children's magazines also offer attractive print material and are a special treat if they come in the mail. In addition to children's literature, print material for adults, including books, magazines, newspapers, and work-related material, should be obvious in the home (Applebee, Langer, & Mullis, 1988; Hannon, 1995).

READING AS A HOME ACTIVITY

Children who are read to regularly by parents, siblings, or other individuals in the home and who have family members who read recreationally become early readers and show a natural interest in books (Bus, van IJzendoorn, & Pellegrini, 1995; Cunningham & Zibulsky, 2014; Sulzby & Teale, 1987). This is not surprising. Through frequent storybook readings, children become familiar with book language and realize the function of written language. Storybook readings are almost always pleasurable, which builds a desire for and interest in reading (Cullinan, 1992; Huck, 1992).

Teachers should encourage family members to read to their children daily. Reading can begin the day a child is born, although an infant's ability to listen attentively is generally limited and varies from one reading to the next. An infant may prefer to chew on the book or pound it rather than listen to it. However, babies read to from birth begin to be attentive in storybook reading situations sooner than those who are not read to (Morrow, 2005). See Appendix D for a checklist for guided participation in reading.

READING TO CHILDREN AT HOME FROM BIRTH TO AGE 8

When babies are read to often, they become responsive to books. From birth to 3 months, a child's attention to book reading is erratic. The baby who stares at the pictures and seems content and quiet can be considered receptive. If the baby wiggles, shows discomfort, or cries, the adult should stop reading and try another time.

From 3 to 6 months, babies become more obviously involved in book readings. They begin to focus on pictures and to listen. Often, they will grab for a book, pound it, and try to put it in their mouth. As long as they seem content, they are involved with the reading.

Six- to 9-month-olds can be purposefully involved in storybook readings. They might try to turn pages, respond to changes in the reader's intonation, or make sounds and movements to demonstrate involvement and pleasure. They sometimes begin to show preferences for books that have been read to them before.

One-year-olds will take a leadership role in turning pages, and they often babble along with the reader in tones that sound like reading. They show strong involvement in being read to; when they see a familiar book, they look for things that they remember from earlier readings such as a brightly colored page.

By 15 months, babies who have been read to can tell which is the front and which is the back of a book, and if the book is right-side up. They begin to identify and name characters in the book. They "read" along with the adult, verbalizing a great deal (Burns, Snow, & Griffin, 1999).

Parents should make reading a ritual; it should be done at the same time and in the same place each day. Bedtime is many children's favorite time to listen to stories and bedtime stories are a good reading habit to establish. Both children and older family members look forward to sharing a book at the end of the day. Reading to children before they go to sleep has a calming effect; it helps establish a routine for children, who can eventually read by themselves before going to bed.

Reading to children should not end when they begin to read themselves. When children are able to read, the bedtime story tradition can evolve into the child's reading to another family member, or it can continue with adults reading aloud books above the reading level of the child. Four- to 7-year-olds are often interested in books with chapters, but are not yet ready to read them on their own. Family members can take this opportunity to motivate young readers by reading aloud more challenging pieces of literature.

Another important way of motivating young readers is to make sure they always have access to new reading material that is of interest to them. Parents should keep track of what their child has read. Adults need to continually put new books in children's hands, even as children grow older and seem to have established the reading habit. Supporting children's reading habits helps children maintain interest in reading.

In addition to reading to their children and reading themselves, families can make a point of providing time for the family to read together. Sitting together around the kitchen table or in the living room, with each family member reading his or her own book, is an enriching activity for all. Talking about what family members are reading is an important experience as well.

STRATEGIES FOR READING AT HOME

Verbal interaction between a family member and child during storybook readings has a major influence on literacy development (Cochran-Smith, 1984; Cunningham & Zibulsky, 2014; Ninio, 1980). When parents interact with their children during storybook reading, they define words, repeat information, and explain ideas, enhancing children's literacy development (Heath, 1982; Morrow, 1987, 2014). Children begin to respond to storybook readings with questions and comments, which become more complex over time as children demonstrate more sophisticated thinking about printed material. Research on home storybook readings has identified a number of interactive behaviors that affect the quality of read-aloud activities. Those behaviors include questioning, scaffolding (modeling dialogue and responses), praising, offering information, directing discussion, sharing personal reactions, and relating concepts to life experiences (Edwards, 1995; Roser & Martinez, 1985; Taylor & Strickland, 1986).

The following discussion (Morrow, 1986) between a mother and her 4-year-old daughter, Natalie, took place at the beginning of a storybook reading and illustrates how an adult can invite and scaffold responses. As a result of her mother's prompts, responses, and support, Natalie pursues her questions and receives additional information.

> MOTHER: Are you ready for our story today, Natalie? This is a new book. I've never read it to you before. It's about a spider that is very busy spinning her web.
>
> NATALIE: Hey, what does that say? (*Points to the title on the front cover.*)
>
> MOTHER: That's called a title. It says "The Very Busy Spider." That's the name of the book. See, it's right here, too: *The Very Busy Spider.*
>
> NATALIE: (*Long pause, then points to the words.*) "The Very Busy Spider"?
>
> MOTHER: Right, you read it. See, you know how to read.
>
> NATALIE: It says, "The Very Busy Spider"? (*Points again with finger.*)
>
> MOTHER: You read it again. Wow, you really know how to read!
>
> NATALIE: Um, now read the book and I'll read it, too.

Natalie's mother reads the story. Each time they come to the text "The spi-der didn't answer. She was very busy spinning her web," she pauses and looks at Natalie, points to the words, and exaggerates her reading of the sentence. After two such episodes, Natalie no longer needs prompting and points and reads along.

FAMILY INVOLVEMENT IN YOUR LITERACY PROGRAM: WHAT TEACHERS CAN DO

Teachers need to view parents as partners in the development of literacy. Every teacher has the responsibility to inform families on a regular basis about what is happening in school and how they can help their child. Teachers need to involve family members in school activities during the day and provide activities for fam-ily members to do at home. Family members need to feel that they are welcome in school; they need opportunities to offer input about what they would like their child to learn, to express how they feel about what happens in school, and to offer suggestions for change.

Long before children enter preschool, teachers need to communicate to fami-lies about the necessity for rich literacy environments. Information can be dissemi-nated at a special meeting for expectant parents; in hospital maternity wards; in obstetrician's and pediatrician's offices; in churches, synagogues, and community agencies. A succinct handout such as Promoting Early Literacy at Home (see Figure 6.1) will be a helpful start and can be printed in different languages found in your community.

WHAT MAKES A LITERACY PROGRAM WITH FAMILY INVOLVEMENT SUCCESSFUL?

Because no two communities are the same, family literacy programs need to be tailored to the needs of the individuals they serve. Figure 6.2 offers some tested tips for program success. At the end of this chapter is a list of resources for teach-ers to share with families. The picture books listed are representative of diverse cultural backgrounds. Each book illustrates a special relationship between family and extended family members.

Family members are children's first and most enduring teachers. Quality pre-schools engage families as an integral part of language and literacy programs— both in school and at home. Reach out to parents and make them an integral part of your reading program.

Your child's ability to read and write depends a lot on the things you do at home from the time he or she is born. The following list suggests materials, activities, and attitudes that are important in helping your child learn to read and write. Check off the things you already do. Then, try to do something on the list that you have not done before.

Materials

_____ Have a space at home for books and magazines for your child.

_____ If you can, subscribe to a magazine for your child.

_____ Keep reading materials on hand for everyone in your home. Visit the library and fill your home with books, magazines, and newspapers for children and adults.

_____ Provide materials that will encourage children to tell or create their own stories, such as puppets, dolls, and audiobooks.

_____ Provide materials for writing, such as crayons, markers, pencils, and paper in different sizes.

Activities

_____ Read or look at books, magazines, or the newspaper with your child. Talk about what you look at or read.

_____ Tell stories together about books, about your family, and about things that you do.

_____ Look at and talk about written material you have such as catalogues, advertisements, work-related materials, and mail.

_____ Provide a model for your child by reading and writing at times when your child can see you.

_____ Write with your child and talk about what you write.

_____ Point out print in your home, such as words on food boxes or recipes, directions on medicine, or instructions on things that require assembly.

_____ Point out print in the neighborhood, such as road signs and names of stores.

_____ Visit the post office, supermarket, or zoo and get books to read about these places. On the way home, talk about what you saw. When you get home, draw and write about the experience.

_____ Use print to communicate with your child. Leave notes for each other. Make to-do lists, grocery lists, and lists for holiday shopping.

(continued)

FIGURE 6.1. Promoting early literacy at home.

Foster Positive Attitudes toward Reading and Writing

_____ Reward your child's attempts at reading and writing, even if they are not perfect, by offering praise. Say kind words like, "What nice work you do," "I'm happy to see you are reading," and "I'm happy to see you are writing. Can I help you?"

_____ Answer your child's questions about reading and writing.

_____ Be sure that reading and writing are enjoyable experiences.

_____ Display your child's work in your home.

_____ Visit school when your child asks. Volunteer to help at school, attend programs in which your child is participating, and attend meetings and family conferences. This lets your child know you care about him or her and school.

FIGURE 6.1. *(continued)*

1. **Communicate goals.** At the beginning of the school year, send home the goals to be achieved in literacy development for the age group you teach in an easy-to-understand format.

2. **Publish a newsletter.** With each new unit of instruction or concept being taught in literacy, send a newsletter to let family members know what you are studying and what they can do to help. Include titles of books they can get from the library to read at home.

3. **Meet with parents.** Invite parents to school programs, parent–teacher conferences, and public meetings about curriculum decisions. Sponsor informational workshops on topics such as reading with children and selecting books to share at home.

4. **Encourage families to assist in the classroom.** Invite parents and grandparents to help with literacy activities such as bookbinding, reading with children, taking written dictation of children's stories, and supervising independent activities while teachers work with small groups and individual children. Whenever parents visit the classroom, encourage them to work with their children. For instance, if parents visit during center time, they can read and write with their children, see what the literacy environment is like at school, and become a more integral part of the child's literacy development.

5. **Send home activities and encourage feedback.** Extend the work you do in the classroom with take-home activities such as reading books aloud, visiting the library, using cookbooks, writing notes, writing in journals together, and watching and talking about programs on television. Whenever you send home activities for parents and children to do together, ask families to provide written feedback about the experience. Such feedback provides insight into what happens at home, holds families accountable for participating, and helps you plan future activities.

6. **Celebrate the families in your classroom.** Invite parents and grandparents to school to share special skills they have, to talk about their cultural heritage, and so forth.

7. **Send home notes when a child is doing well.** Don't wait to send notes just when problems arise.

8. **Provide lists of literature for family members to share with their children.** (Appendix A suggests books on a variety of topics.)

9. **Include family members in helping to assess their child's progress.** Provide forms for family members to fill out about their child's literacy activities and things they do with their child at home. Have them contribute information about their child's progress at parent conferences.

FIGURE 6.2. Tips for promoting parent involvement in the preschool literacy program.

PROFESSIONAL DEVELOPMENT FOR PRE- AND INSERVICE TEACHERS

Make a strong effort to include parents in your program. Have parents come to school for an information session and model good storybook reading for them, identify good characteristics of children's literature, and make suggestions of good children's literature to read to their children. Help them to understand the importance of exposure to many genres. Model storytelling with and without props for parents. Have parents make a story prop to bring home. Have parents complete the form in Figure 6.3 so you have some insight as to what parents are doing with children at home and what your children are doing with literature at home. Let your parents know about themes being studied and invite them to read a book about the theme. If they have books from other countries, they are welcome to read them in their own language if they wish. The teacher can read it first in English.

Check the list of tips for family literacy programs in Figure 6.4 and see how many of the suggested activities you do. Try new ones and reflect with your peers on how they worked out. Finally, create a plan for your own professional development that deals with enhancing your knowledge about using children's literature and developing comprehension skills in preschool.

CONCLUSION

It is crucial to involve families in the school literacy program. Children are with their parents more than with teachers. We need to involve parents in school programs so they see what we do with their children. We need to offer suggestions about what they can do with their children at home to enhance literacy. Teachers cannot be the only source of literacy in a child's life. Parents need to have books for their children at home and to read to them often. With home support, children will be able to reach their full potential in literacy development.

Preschool in Practice

HIGHLIGHTING FAMILY INVOLVEMENT AT SCHOOL

Every month in our school several family involvement activities occur. These activities provide opportunities for children to bond with their own families and other families and to share their diverse cultural backgrounds with their classmates. To emphasize the importance of these activities and others, teachers in all grades began a showcase called "Highlighting Family Involvement." They keep cameras in school so that, when families participate, the teachers can take their pictures for the showcase. The following are the activities at school that help fill the showcase and bring families to the building:

Checklist: Observing My Child's Literacy Growth

Child's Name: _____

Date: _____

	Always	Sometimes	Never	Comments
1. My child asks to be read to.				
2. My child will read or look at a book alone.				
3. My child understands what is read to him or her, or what he or she reads to him- or herself.				
4. My child handles a book properly, knows how to turn pages, and knows that print is read from left to right.				
5. My child will pretend to read or read to me.				
6. My child participates in the reading of a story, with rhymes and repeated phrases.				
7. My child will write with me.				
8. My child will write alone.				
9. My child will talk about what he or she has written.				
10. My child reads print in the environment, such as sign and labels.				
11. My child likes school.				
Comments about your child:				

FIGURE 6.3. Child progress information form. From Morrow (1988b). Copyright 1988 by the International Reading Association. Reprinted by permission.

- Respect and understand the diversity of the families you serve.
- Be aware of the different languages used in children's homes within the community. Translate materials so that everyone can understand them.
- Accommodate all schedules by holding meetings at varied times of the day and days of the week.
- Provide transportation if family members do not have a way of getting to meetings.
- Provide child care at meetings.
- Serve food and refreshments.
- At family meetings, offer ideas and materials that families can share at home.
- Encourage family members' participation in school activities during school hours.

FIGURE 6.4. Tips for family literacy programs.

Theme Nights

These evenings are devoted to different topics, such as other countries, where children and families can learn together. Families share artifacts and then read, write, and do art projects about the theme.

Cooking Nights

Families bring easy favorite recipes to share and make together. The best part is eating the goodies when the cooking is done.

Book-Sharing Evenings

Everyone brings a favorite book and reads or tells about his or her favorite part. The book can be in another language and, if necessary, a translator is used so that everyone can participate.

Sharing Family Photos

On this night we ask everyone to bring family pictures they want to share. We talk and write about them. Each family makes an album with the photos, and we encourage them to continue to fill the album they started at school.

Themed-Based Reading and Writing Backpacks

For this activity Ms. Corona assembled a themed-based backpack with the following materials: a class journal; a book that represented the theme being studied; and a folder with songs, poems, or experiments related to the theme and related links to videos. The children take the backpack home on a rotating basis for a few days. The parents and children are told to share the activities and books with their family. Model some of the activities at Back to School Night and talk about the backpack at parent conferences. With their parents children are to dictate things about what is happening in school to the parent who writes it in the class journal. Read the book in the backpack, and sing the songs, or read the poems and do the experiments or art project suggested.

CHILDREN'S LITERATURE CITED IN THIS CHAPTER

The Very Busy Spider by Eric Carle (1985). Philomel Books.
The Very Hungry Caterpillar by Eric Carle (1994). Philomel Books.

FAMILY LITERACY RESOURCES FOR PARENTS AND EDUCATORS

International Reading Association. (1997). *Explore the playground of books: Tips for parents of beginning readers* [Brochure]. Newark, DE: Author.

International Reading Association. (1997). *Get ready to read! Tips for parents of young children* [Brochure]. Newark, DE: Author.

International Reading Association. (1999). *Beginning literacy and your child: A guide to helping your baby or preschooler become a reader* [Booklet]. Newark, DE: Author.

Lipson, E. R. (2000). *New York Times parent's guide to the best books for children.* New York: Crown.

National Association for the Education of Young Children. (2004). *Raising a reader, raising a writer: How parents can help* [Brochure]. Washington, DC: Author.

Trelease, J. (1985). *The read-aloud handbook.* New York: Penguin.

IDEAS FOR DISCUSSION, REFLECTION, AND ACTION

1. Have parents come to school for an information session about literacy development. Model good storybook reading for them, and identify characteristics of good children's literature. Provide the parents with the names of stories they should read to their children. Let them know about the themes being studied in school and invite them to read a book about the theme to the class.

2. Create an activity for parents that is not discussed in this chapter. Describe it to another teacher and discuss how you could carry out this plan together.

3. Encourage parents to come to school to observe and participate in the classroom. For example, they might observe the teacher reading a story to the children, or help with a dramatic play period in centers that encourage reading and writing, or participate in an art experience when children are working on a theme-based project. Soon after, invite the parents back to school to discuss what they saw. Explain the importance of the observed activities and answer any questions the parents have.

4. Each month, send home an activity for parents to do with their child. Every activity should have an accountability measure to determine if it was done. For example, once a month, ask the parents to read a story to their child, discuss it with him or her, and then have the child illustrate anything about the story. This illustration should be brought to school for a classroom discussion with the teacher. For another activity, ask the parent and child to keep a journal together. Once a month, both the parent and child write something in the journal. When it is their turn, ask the parent to send in the journal so the teacher can see what they are writing.

CHAPTER 7

Putting It All Together
in the Early Childhood Classroom

In real early childhood classrooms, literacy learning does not occur apart from other early learning domains. Rather, it is integrated into the full fabric of early education and care. Many preschool classrooms follow an integrated school day, in which skills from all content areas are taught within the context of a topic of study. In an interdisciplinary approach, topics are drawn from children's interests and experiences. Learning experiences are socially interactive and process oriented, giving children time to explore and experiment with varied materials.

What follows is a slice of life taken from 1 day in one preschool teacher's classroom. What we hope to show is how this teacher brings the joining framework of language and literacy to life for the whole child. If you look carefully you will see how the teacher weaves the literacy skills in with the procedures. The teacher is Sheila Madison, and her teaching assistant is Maria Rivera. Maria completed her child development associate credential and is currently enrolled in a 2-year early childhood program at the local community college. This year, Sheila and Maria have a class of 20 preschoolers (13 girls, 7 boys), 6 of whom are African American, 3 of Middle Eastern descent, 10 of European American descent, and 1 of Asian descent.

BEFORE THE EVERYDAY ROUTINE BEGINS

Sheila recently attended a workshop on the early learning content standards, so she knows she has to spend time planning and making materials that will help children achieve standards-based performance indicators in language and literacy. Therefore, the everyday routine for children in Sheila's preschool classroom begins with lots of preplanning and behind-the-scenes preparation.

Even before the preschool program officially started, she set up the physical environment as a place for her young children to play, learn, and have fun with friends. She organized the space and arranged the furniture in an inviting way. She used signage with complementary graphics to present information in easy-to-read ways that appeal to children (and are located within their line of sight). She took stock of her resources, including the size of her read-aloud collection (about 350 mixed-genre books), and reviewed the records of the children she will teach. She made "starter" name tags (to be completed by the children with their own "mark") and prepared essential charts for initial routines (e.g., the sign-in chart). After this initial preparation, Sheila knows she will need to commit substantial time every day to planning for instruction across the program year.

THE START OF THE DAY

A typical day begins as children hang up their coats or sweaters (with a little help from the adults) and then proceed to unpack and sort the contents of their book bags into one of two boxes located on a low table outside the preschool door. One box is labeled "Take-Home Books" with a photo of books. This is where children return the books they took home the night before. The other is labeled "Take-Home Folders" with a photo of folders. Here they return their home folder, which is one way Sheila stays in close communication with parents and caregivers.

Today, she is particularly pleased to see that Mina, who has recently arrived from Morocco, is able to put her books in the "Take-Home Books" box and her folder in the "Take-Home Folders" box. Having this routine to follow seems to have made Mina more comfortable in the classroom. Finally, the children put their names on the sign-in chart just inside the door, letting everyone know "I'm here today!" For Sheila and her teacher assistant, Maria, the daily routine of signing in provides ongoing monitoring of children's name-writing skills: What alphabet letters they know and how well they can form them on paper. Mina's mother showed Sheila how to write Mina's name in Arabic. Sheila placed Mina's name in Arabic and in English over her cubby. Now Mina is working on writing her name using the English alphabet.

Sheila starts with children's names rather than a letter of the week because she knows that a child's own name is one of the best sources of alphabet knowledge for children, and that writing the initial letter of the child's name develops phoneme sensitivity (Bus & Both-de Vries, 2008). Moreover, if James knows that *J* is the first letter in his name, he might recognize it somewhere else in the preschool learning environment—on the felt board, in a book, on a chart, or in another child's name printed neatly on a cubby.

Sheila purposefully watches for children's letter-name and sound recognition in a variety of activities that center on their name writing. From these activities, all the children learn one another's names and the first letter that starts one another's names. At the same time, these activities give the children the opportunity to play with the sound that a letter makes, to feel the sound of each letter with their mouths and tongues, and to think of other words (real or made up) that also start with the same sound.

After signing in, the children move to tables and browse books or put puzzles together until all the others arrive. Easing into the day in this social way gives children a chance to greet each other ("Hi, Sheona, my mommy bringed me today. Did you know?"), share happenings ("My Auntie JoJo is comin' for a real long time. She lives in Chicago"), discuss what they see in the books they're reading ("Hey, Alex. Is this a dinosaur? Is this a pterodactyl?"), or work together to assemble a puzzle ("These is easy for us, right? Everythin's easy for us"). Sheila uses this time, too, to casually converse with the children one on one. When she stops at the table where Mina is working on a puzzle, she crouches down and says, "I see you have a puzzle, Mina. There are dogs and cats and mice and birds in your puzzle," pointing to each type of animal as she names them. Although Mina does not say anything to Sheila, she watches her teacher's face intently as she names the puzzle pieces. After Sheila leaves, Mina says some of the words softly to herself: "Dog, bird. . . ."

AND NOW IT'S TIME FOR THE MORNING MEETING

Clap, clap, sing, song, snap, snap! The Morning Meeting opens with songs, rhymes, and finger plays. Sheila introduces a new rhyme every week, but soon the children beg to open with their favorites every day—just for the sheer delight of saying or singing the words and sounds. Sheila, however, is quite deliberate about using this fun with songs, chants, and rhymes to build the phonological awareness of her preschoolers. She knows that their active engagement in singing, rhyming, and chanting helps them learn to listen for the sounds in language. Last week during Morning Meeting time, Sheila noticed that Mina was joining in the rhymes for the first time. In fact, this was the first time that Sheila had heard Mina's voice in the classroom. Today, Mina wears a big smile as she shouts out the chants with the rest of the class.

After this warm-up activity, the schedule reader points to each event on the day's schedule while the rest of the group reads along. As they go, Sheila guides them to vary their volume as they chorally read, sometimes soft as snowflakes falling to the ground and sometimes loud like drums in a parade. The children are eager to explore the sounds of their own voices along with the printed words of the schedule.

The children settle and Sheila begins the shared reading session. The book today is the Big Book version of *Curious George* (Rey, 1941), a story about a mischievous monkey. Before reading, she engages the children's interest in the story and points out the particulars of title, author, and illustrator. She takes a picture walk through the story, pointing out the illustrations, highlighting key points and interesting new words. Then she reads, and as she goes she engages the children.

> "What do you think will happen? How do you know that? This word is *curious*. You say it: *curious*. It means to be very interested in something. Turn and tell your friend what it means. Isn't that a funny word? Look at how it looks, so long with so many letters in it. Did I see an *s* in there by any chance? I'm a bit worried about George, aren't you? Well, now, wasn't that a great story? It reminds me of our field trip to the zoo a while back where we saw monkeys scampering and playing. What does it remind you of? Before we leave this story, today, let's do a picture walk again. This time, you help me out and we can retell this story."

On another day, Sheila will use a different after-reading activity, such as building vocabulary, reconstructing the story with sequence cards, reviewing the rhyming words in the book, or beginning a letter- or word-matching activity. Sheila consciously varies the genres she reads to the children, and uses Big Book versions when available. Sometimes selections are stories and old favorites. The group adores *Lilly's Purple Plastic Purse* (Henkes, 2006) and *The Napping House* (Wood, 2000). At other times, she uses informational books that develop vocabulary and basic concepts, such as *Cats* (Gibbons, 1996), *Ducks Don't Get Wet* (Goldin, 1965), and *Spiders* (Resnick, 1996). To help children remember new words, she regularly discusses them with the children before, during, and after reading. She has them dramatize informational books to help them remember ideas, terms, and facts.

Morning Meeting time draws to a close with the question of the day: "Did you enjoy yesterday's program with Max the moose?" The children respond with a resounding "Yes!" They then take turns bringing up a clothespin labeled with their name and attaching it to the "Yes" side of the chart. However, the results for yesterday's question, "Do you like chocolate milk?" were not unanimous, with 15 "Yes" votes and a surprising six "No" votes. As children post their votes, they slide their finger under Yes or No as they say it. Today, for the first time, Mina not only places her name on the chart but also says the word aloud: "Yes!" With Sheila's assistance, the children discuss today's results, which involves much talk and saying the word *unanimous*.

The children huddle around Sheila and Maria to share their play plans. They use the Play Area Chart to remind them where they played yesterday and to decide where they will start for the day. Several boys say they want to play in the block area, but Sheila reminds them that they have played there a lot, so maybe today they should try a new area. "How about the discovery area at the sand table where you can make wide roads and build tunnels with your bulldozers and dump trucks?" She turns to a few girls, encouraging them to think about the art area where they can make play props for the Health Foods Shop currently set up in the dramatic play area. Maria nods to Savannah. "Thank you, Savannah, for helping Mina choose the Health Foods Shop today." As the children finalize their decisions, they take their name tags to the play area of their choice.

James, Andrea, Mina, and Amanda head off for the dramatic play area, which is set up as a Health Foods Shop to further the current theme of "Healthy You, Healthy Me." Grocery packages, cookbooks, a "new healthy foods" demonstration area, recipes, notepads, coupons, and writing tools are available for play scenarios about cooking, food groups, and healthy eating. Sheila knows that the play talk that goes on here develops children's use of decontextualized language and provides opportunities for them to use new words, such as *fats*, *carbohydrates*, *proteins*, and *calories*. For the play to unfold, the children must listen to one another. As the children play, they are exposed to the culture, customs, and background knowledge of their friends. Although Mina does not add any talk to the play, she is a willing participant and listens carefully to the other children as they develop their play themes.

Jamal, Nicholas, and Blair head for the block/truck construction area where there are all kinds of books on construction, as well as paper and pencils to take work orders and a set of blueprints for reference. Another group moves toward the writing table, stocked with all manner of writing supplies such as stencils, pens, pencils, envelopes, tactile letters, and different kinds of paper. Other materials are purposefully placed to provide practice with recognizing alphabet letters, making writing attempts, matching and sorting sounds, and other activities related to this week's objectives, which are as follows:

- Use new, topic-related words during play.
- Express ideas through drawing and writing.

- Play and manipulate sounds in words by saying, pronouncing, and sorting.
- Recognize alphabet letters in own name.

Sheona, Jaclyn, Isaiah, and Josie move to the book area because they like to play school. Today they will read and manipulate several interactive charts. "Little Miss Muffet" is especially popular because of that scary word: *spider*! After a few squeamish rounds with the word *spider*, the group splits with some children inserting picture cards of other creatures into the Miss Muffet chart and others exploring different charts with familiar nursery rhymes, songs, and chants.

Sheila and Maria circulate among the play areas with several goals in mind. For brief periods, they may engage a few children in small-group instruction on a specific skill, such as hearing rhymes in words. Or each of them may involve one or more children in a read-aloud. At other times, they model language and play behaviors as needed. They support children's efforts and play along at their direction. While the children are deeply immersed in the flow of play, the teachers also informally assess the children's use of language and early literacy skills.

Bringing an end to playtime, the teachers lead the children out the door to the playground for some time in the sunshine. They introduce a game—Duck, Duck, Goose—to the children. Sheila is pleased to see that Mina is an active participant in this game, as it had been difficult at first getting her involved in games. Today, she is as eager as the other children to take her turn, touching each child and saying "Duck," until she comes to the one she wants to pick as the "Goose." After a few rounds, Sheila asks Jared to follow her lead, which he does with a voice of great authority.

BREAK FOR A SNACK

The children assemble for snack time. Today, like every day, Sheila and Maria set out the snack with a sign that tells "How Many" snack items each child should count out and enjoy. The numeral is clearly written, followed by dots that children can count. The teachers are deliberately building children's math skills by handling snack time in this way. Children count to 10, touch objects, and say the number names. Identifying and naming numerals, and demonstrating a one-to-one correspondence when counting are important early learning math content standards addressed during this simple snack-counting routine.

Conversations flow as the teachers pose questions about the snack ("These baby carrots are crunchy, don't you think?"), prompt the sharing of preferences or similar foods served at home ("Elijah, you were telling me once that your grandma makes the best carrot cake. Is that right?"), and talk about what play centers the children played in today ("I was wondering, Rosa and Spencer, if you fixed a lot of cars today?").

ONE MORE READ-ALOUD BEFORE THE CLOSE OF THE DAY

After their healthy snack of carrots, raisins, wheat crackers, and apple juice, the children gather for another read-aloud. One small group joins Sheila, and another goes with Maria. Today is the second read of *Raccoon on His Own* (Arnosky, 2003) with Sheila and of *Knuffle Bunny* (Willems, 2004) with Maria. This time, the children will add details to the story problem, tell portions aloud, and ask why questions, such as "Why is Daddy mad at Trixie?" (in *Knuffle Bunny*) or "Why is he [raccoon] scared?" (in *Raccoon on His Own*). After a third read on another day, the pair will rotate groups, so all of the children have the chance to participate interactively in both stories. Sheila is considering using a story drama technique with her group as a way to reenact the story (Charters & Gately, 1986). She likes this technique because it helps the children become acquainted with the plot structure of the story: setting, the problem, the buildup of tension, the turning point, and finally the resolution.

ENDING THE DAY

It is nearly time to depart, so the children all gather as Sheila passes around the Mystery Box for the children to explore. They put their hands in the box: "So, what do you think it is? What does it feel like? Tell me some more. Savannah said it felt like it had ridges. What do you think she meant?" The children feel with their hands and talk. "It feels like a round thing. Does it go on our trucks? It has hard spots." They listen intently for more clues. All the while, Sheila knows that she is helping the children learn to listen, to use descriptive words, and to express their thinking with language.

She continues to encourage talk for a short bit and then turns to the easel for some writing. "Let's record this mystery," she says, and she begins to write what the children have to say. Alex says, "It feels like a round thing." Sheila talks about the words as she writes, "It is a short word and I hear a /t/ at the end. I need to leave a space before I start to write *feels*." She finishes the sentence and then takes another suggestion from the children. After three or four sentences, the children have enough clues to identify the mystery object—a small tire that fell off one of the tractors in the block area. "We were looking for that tire for a long time," Isaiah says. Missing object found and mystery solved! At the completion of this whole-class time, children choose take-home books, get their mail, and then go to their cubbies and pack their backpacks for dismissal.

TODAY AND THEREAFTER

After the children have gone, Sheila and Maria tidy up the room and then turn to an accounting of the day. Today, like every day, they use their progress monitoring tools to keep track of how children are doing in terms of instructional goals. Sheila writes up her anecdotal notes, while Maria collects work samples, like language experience stories that children have dictated during the day. Later these items are posted to each child's "working" portfolio. In addition, they conduct a 5-Minute Friday Conference every week with three or four children who need more support. Based on the weekly objectives, they check these children's letter-name knowledge, knowledge of vocabulary words, and rhyming and alliteration skills. In these routine ways, the pair keeps track of the children's language development and early literacy learning and monitor the effectiveness of their own instruction.

LITERATURE, LITERACY, SCIENCE, AND SOCIAL STUDIES IN PRESCHOOL THEMES

Science and social studies are probably the two content areas that provide the greatest opportunities for literacy development because topics in these subject areas typically generate enthusiasm and a purpose for reading and writing. For instance, a unit about the farm can promote oral language development through discussions about farm work, different types of farms, and farm animals. Children can generate word lists of farm animals, crops, and jobs. Pictures of farm scenes, a trip to a farm, or a visit by a farmer generate discussion, reading, and writing. By reading picture books about farms to the class, teachers can encourage positive attitudes toward books, enhance children's vocabulary, and share information about farming. *The Milk Makers* (Gibbons, 1987), *Barn Dance!* (Hutchins, 2007), and *My Trip to the Farm* (Mayer, 2002) are just a few children's classics that deal with rural life. *Big Red Barn* (Brown, 1995) features rhymed text and illustrations introducing the different animals that live on a farm. Children will enjoy picking up the books on their own, sharing them with friends, and retelling and role-playing the stories. A farm visit can be retold in stories or drawings and then be bound into class books. Science and social studies are probably the two content areas that provide the greatest opportunities for literacy development because topics in these subject areas typically generate enthusiasm and a purpose for reading and writing.

Science experiments and food preparation offer other opportunities for discussion and vocabulary enrichment. Whether the topic is the weather or plants, collections of books that are both informational and narrative can be provided to enhance and expand the child's knowledge of the world.

LITERATURE, LITERACY, AND ART IN PRESCHOOL THEMES

Art experiences allow children to explore and experiment with interesting materials such as finger paints and watercolors; colored pencils, felt-tip markers, and crayons; construction paper, tissue paper, foil, and transparent wrap; and paste, scissors, clay, and play dough. To link art and literacy within a theme, teachers can instruct children to create theme-related pictures. For example, after reading the book *Autumn* (Saunders-Smith, 1998), the class can discuss fruits and colors of fall and then make pictures using colors such as yellow, orange, green, brown, and red. Some children will make representational drawings; others will do scribble drawings. All are acceptable. The pictures can be fastened together to make a fall book.

Discussing children's book illustrators and illustration styles is a natural way of linking art and literature for young children. For example, Betsy Lewin, illustrator of *Giggle, Giggle, Quack* (Cronin, 2002) and *Click, Clack, Moo: Cows That Type* (Cronin, 2000), used a variety of different brushes to illustrate characters and emotions. Leo Lionni, author and illustrator of *Frederick* (1973), created some of his artwork using crayons. Eric Carle, author and illustrator of *The Very Hungry Caterpillar* (2007) and *The Very Busy Spider* (1985), writes mostly about animals and insects. He uses bright colors and his art has a distinctive, bold style.

Young children can learn to distinguish some of the techniques of well-known illustrators and talk about how they are similar or different. They can select materials used by these illustrators for their own pictures.

LITERATURE, LITERACY, AND MUSIC IN PRESCHOOL THEMES

Music provides abundant opportunities for literacy development. Songs introduce children to new words and word patterns, expanding their vocabularies and building their *phonological awareness*. When songs are written on charts and teachers point to the words to track the print across the page, children learn important print concepts.

Songs based on current topics of study are an essential element of the preschool curriculum, and books based on songs are a great addition to any classroom library. When studying farms, for example, select books to feature such as *Old McDonald Had a Farm* (Cabrera, 2008) and *Go Tell Aunt Rhody* (Quackenbush, 1973). You can read the words and sing the songs with children. Many holiday songs have been adapted into books: *Over the River and Through the Wood* (Child, 1999) and *Five Little Pumpkins* (Van Rynbach, 1995) are two popular examples. Listening to music inspires children to form mental images about a theme. For this reason, music is a rich source for generating descriptive language. Ask children to close their eyes while listening to the music and think about the theme they are studying. Ask them to describe images that come to mind.

LITERATURE, LITERACY, AND MATH IN PRESCHOOL THEMES

Math and literacy are not incompatible. Math-related storybooks introduce young children to numeracy concepts and extend their math vocabulary. The following are just a few of the excellent math storybooks available for the preschool classroom:

- Bang, M. (1991). *Ten, nine, eight.* New York: HarperCollins.
- Ehlert, L. (1992). *Fish eyes.* San Diego, CA: Harcourt.
- Grossman, B. (1998). *My little sister ate one hare.* New York: Random House.
- Roth, C. (2002). *Ten dirty pigs, ten clean pigs.* New York: North-South.

Children ask for the skills they need to understand content information because they have an interest in it (Manning, Manning, & Long, 1994; Walmsley, 1994). For example, during a discussion of a transportation theme in Suzanne's kindergarten class, children asked for even more materials than she had already made available in the several centers. Books on transportation led to requests for books on space travel and various maps of places. The interesting experiences provided for the children made them eager to learn more.

CONDUCTING A THEMATIC UNIT

Theme topics can be selected by the teacher and the children. Giving students choices concerning what they will learn is important. When a topic is selected, invite the children to brainstorm what they would like to know about (RAND Reading Study Group, 2002). To gain a better understanding of the role of literature in a thematic unit, consider the following example from a preschool unit on "animals around the world." Although the unit includes activities for all content areas, here we examine only the activities that involve children's literature.

Preparing for the Unit

To begin the theme on animals around the world, prepare the room so that the theme is evident to those who enter your classroom. Add new, theme-related materials to all classroom areas, including the literacy center. For example, in the *writing center*, you can include animal-shaped blank books and a message board on which to share the Morning Message. In the library corner, you can include storybooks and informational texts on animals as well as pamphlets and magazines about animal habitat. A list of animal-related picture books can be found in Appendix A.

Activities for the Theme

The following activities are initiated through the use of children's literature. Each relates to the theme "animals around the world."

Literacy

Objective: Create an alphabet book that reviews many animal words learned in the unit.

Procedure: An "Amazing Animal Alphabet Book" will be made and photocopied for each child in the class. Each letter will represent a different animal (e.g., *A*, armadillo; *B*, bird; *C*, chimpanzee; *D*, dog; *E*, elephant; *F*, fish). The students will read the letters and words with the teacher and each other.

Art

Objective: Participate in a creative art activity related to a storybook that includes learning about animal faces.

Procedure: After reading the book *Animal Faces* (Satoh & Toda, 1996), discuss the similarities and differences among various animal faces. Provide students with materials such as paper plates, crayons, construction paper, macaroni, and feathers to make their own zoo face masks. A piece of string can be tied to either side to fit the mask around their heads.

Music

Objective: Identify vocabulary for animal names by singing theme-related songs.

Procedure: A collection of animal songs can be found in *Wee Sing, Animals, Animals, Animals* (Beall & Nipp, 2006). Sing the songs found in the book. On a large piece of paper list the animals mentioned and have the children copy the words in a writing journal.

Science

Objective: Discuss the metamorphosis of a caterpillar into a butterfly. Read the story and have students draw pictures and write words to demonstrate comprehension.

Procedure: Read the book *My, Oh My—A Butterfly! All About Butterflies* (Rabe, 2007) to learn about the metamorphosis of a caterpillar. Students can draw pictures and add corresponding vocabulary words to illustrate the miraculous transformation.

Social Studies

Objective: Match the animals with their country of origin. Become more familiar with world geography.

Procedure: Have children color pictures of adult and baby animals and paste on construction paper. Display a map of the world for students to paste the animal in the appropriate region. The book *Animal Homes* (Chessen & Chanko, 1998) will help students develop content knowledge.

Math

Objective: Use math vocabulary when retelling a story. Match numbers and objects.

Procedure: Read a story related to animals such as *1, 2, 3 to the Zoo: A Counting Book* (Carle, 1998). Ask the class to retell the story using props for the animals that are in the book. Have children count the different types of animals on each page of the book and match the numeral to the corresponding animal.

TEACHERS CONTINUE TO LEARN, TOO

Teachers depend on many kinds of knowledge to meet their responsibilities of helping young children gain oral language and early literacy as first steps in school readiness. Today's teachers and teacher assistants not only must be able to create stimulating and orderly early learning environments, but they also must help diverse groups of children learn more complex content and develop a wider range of oral language and early literacy skills. For this, initial preparation is not enough nor can experience alone supply adequate knowledge and skills. To be successful teachers and teacher assistants, early educators need to engage in ongoing professional learning to add to their knowledge and skills across their careers.

Learning about Young Children

Teachers and teacher assistants are busy people, and the time they spend in professional development must be time well spent. Priority should be given to learning more about young learners and how they develop. School readiness in the early years involves the whole child. To be effective, early childhood professionals need to be able to support children's development across different growth areas that interact with one another, including physical, socioemotional, and cognitive domains. The growing diversity of families and children also requires understanding cultural differences that may make a difference in children's development.

To help all children learn language and literacy, early childhood educators need to be prepared to recognize the unique ways each child has learned to learn and to support each child's learning needs for language and literacy growth. Teachers and their assistants need to know about language development, including second-language acquisition—and to be especially concerned with promoting children's communication skills and building their store of vocabulary.

Learning More about Curriculum

Teachers and teacher assistants need to know about early learning content standards at the national, state, and local levels because these provide the general guidelines about what to teach and why. Time must be given to learning how to read and interpret standards frameworks, how to use them in planning, and how to approach them with particular groups of children.

More than ever before, teachers are faced with making curriculum decisions about oral language and early literacy materials for their classrooms. How well do these new material resources meet the standards? Are they research based? Are they appropriate for these children in this community? How well do they fit into our program? How do they support youngsters at risk? Questions like these require teachers to develop a curricular vision that keeps standards-based goals *and* developmentally appropriate instruction in sight when making decisions about materials and instructional approaches. In the end, the best preschool program is one constructed by teachers in response to adopted standards, particular needs and prior experiences of the children, and the resources and demands of the local community. Strong preschool language and literacy programs are assembled and built, not bought wholesale and applied.

Learning More about Skillful Teaching

To provide effective oral language instruction that supports early literacy, teachers and their assistants need to cultivate an ever-deepening understanding of how young children make sense of (and also confuse) language and literacy concepts. Knowing that most 4-year-olds hold a very fragile sense of word, for example, underlies effective instruction in the alphabetic principle at this age.

Further, teachers in collaboration with their assistants must apply effective practices to meet a wide range of diverse learning needs among young children, which involves constructing a culturally responsive curriculum, as well as an inclusive one. To help young learners with all their many differences acquire common, high-level oral language and early literacy concepts and skills, teachers need to be skilled assessors who can use many different assessment tools. They must command a repertoire of formative assessment strategies, including ways to help young children acquire self-regulation skills. For all this to happen day in and day out, teachers must be fluent in sound classroom management techniques and well organized to ensure a productive learning environment.

VENUES FOR PROFESSIONAL LEARNING

Fortunately, opportunities for professional learning in early literacy abound these days and are increasingly accessible to early childhood educators everywhere. You may be fortunate enough to become involved in a federal program, like Early

Reading First, or a large-scale study sponsored through the National Institute of Child Health and Human Development (2000). You may choose to enroll in a professional education program to gain a new credential or degree. (Many find this an attractive route because it can lead to new job opportunities.)

Then there is an ever-growing menu of learning options online. You can take an online course, such as those offered through PBS Teacher Line (*www.pbs.org/ teacherline*).

Professional organizations, such as the National Association for the Education of Young Children (NAEYC) and the International Reading Association (IRA), also provide conference opportunities for learning where you can attend workshop sessions, discuss hot topics with colleagues, and purchase top-notch professional books for your own personal learning.

Of course, your own workplace is also a place where you can participate in periodic training workshops and study groups. Why not start a book club and choose a professional book to read and discuss every month?

No matter the venue, the important point is that you continue to learn about young children's language and literacy development and apply this knowledge to your own continuous improvement as an early literacy teacher. An effective professional development program should have the following characteristics (adapted from Hawley & Valli, 1999):

- Connects content and activities to standards of early learning.
- Provides opportunities to practice new skills.
- Models specific instructional techniques to use.
- Builds a community of early educators.
- Includes a follow-up to support classroom practice.

We have one last piece of advice before you close this book: When making decisions about how to spend your time learning, keep these characteristics of quality professional development in mind. You are worth it.

CONCLUSION

Good teaching takes a great deal of planning. Children need a daily routine they can count on. They also need to be engaged in relevant and meaningful activities. Themes help to make the curriculum both relevant and meaningful. Embedding literacy throughout the school day, when doing science, social studies, math, art, music, and play is advisable because literacy is of the utmost importance to develop throughout preschool. Teachers need to stay on top of the past, the present, and new ideas. Professional development is necessary to enhance teaching methods. The chapter began with a visit into Sheila and Maria's preschool classroom, if only for a short time. We learned from their example that preschool teachers and teacher assistants, working together, can nurture young children's early literacy development. As a result, all young children grow more capable in their abilities to talk, read, and write—and to flourish in school.

Preschool in Practice

PLANNING AND DESIGNING CURRICULUM WITH THE END IN MIND

Collaborate with other teachers in your school regularly to design and plan a 6- to 8-week in-depth topic studies for implementation in classrooms. If it is fall in the school year, for example, design a topic study of *seeds* for the spring term. Be sure that what you plan is purposeful, challenging, and is a content-rich activity at the heart of learning experiences that develop children's language, content vocabulary, and literacy knowledge. A study of seeds offers many opportunities for firsthand exploration, as well as shared reading, writing, and talking.

Begin your design process with the end in mind (Wiggins & McTighe, 2005). Ask yourself "What are the desired results? What should children be able to do with what they learn about seeds on their own?" Consult early learning content standards to identify a set of expectations for the unit, including language and literacy, mathematics, and science goals. Keep this a manageable, doable set of expectations that can be addressed in a 6- to 8-week time frame. Identify a few big ideas that will help children make sense of their experiences; ideas that will help them to "connect the dots." State these in simple terms, such as "There are many different kinds of seeds. Seeds grow into plants with roots, stems, leaves, and flowers." From this foundation they generate essential questions to stimulate children's interest and to guide their study. One of their favorite questions is (in child-friendly terms): "Why do plants grow up, not down?" Finally, decide on specific knowledge, skills, and dispositions that will focus instructional activities on learning language, literacy, and content vocabulary (e.g., record observations of seed growth using print and pictures).

Consider what evidence you will collect and use to monitor and evaluate children's progress. You can use informal checks, direct observations, prompts (writing, drawing), and extended projects (e.g., sprouting seeds and keeping a record of observations). Develop a small set of informal assessments for determining children's knowledge of seeds and seed growth, their ability to use language to communicate what they know and to collaborate with others, their print knowledge and skills for reading and writing about seeds, and their active participation in activities. You could also create rubrics for some of the assessments so that your observations of children's performance would be consistent across classrooms.

Designing Activities for the Curriculum with the End in Mind

List activities to engage children in a long-term study of seeds. All activities should help children (1) acquire the basic knowledge and skills they need for understanding the topic, (2) make meaning of big ideas and expectations, and (3) transfer what they know and can do to other situations (e.g., helping to plant a garden at home or in their neighborhood). One excellent activity is to make a Silly Birdseed Garden.

Settings and Props

Equip the area with sponges, birdseed, and clipboards with markers for labeling and sketching.

Procedure

1. Prepare the children by previewing what they will do. Post a chart that shows how to make a Silly Birdseed Garden.
   - Step 1: Soak birdseed in water overnight.
   - Step 2: Sprinkle seed on a damp sponge.
   - Step 3: Put the sponge in a warm, dark spot until seeds sprout.
   - Step 4: Move sponge into the sun.
   - Step 5: Watch the seeds grow!
2. Explain that the gardens will be "planted" in the greenhouse (the new name for the discovery play area) during center time.
3. Rotate children through the play area in groups of three or four over several days. Ask them to make predictions about what they will see in their gardens. Record some of their predictions on chart paper and post for all to read.
4. Ask the children to label their gardens and put them in a dark cupboard in the greenhouse until they have germinated. Once the seeds sprout, have them sketch what they observe. Remind them to check their predictions.
5. Place the growing gardens in the windowsill garden. Have marking sticks and hand magnifiers available for children to examine and record the growth of their *silly* gardens.

When the gardens grow have a garden party for parents, grandparents, and school staff. Make and deliver invitations, serve seed candy, sing songs about seeds and flowers, display seed art, and show off beautiful mini-gardens.

Designing with the end in mind (not rushing to activities) can be very challenging, but it also can be very rewarding not only for teacher collaboration and learning, but also for engaging young children in worthwhile learning activities that transfer to new learning situations.

CHILDREN'S LITERATURE CITED IN THIS CHAPTER

Animal Faces by Akira Satoh and Kyoko Toda (1996). Miller.
Animal Homes by Betsey Chessen and Pamela Chanko (1998). Scholastic.
Autumn by Gail Saunders-Smith (1998). Capstone Press.
Barn Dance! by Pat Hutchins (2007). Greenwillow Books.
Big Red Barn by Margaret Wise Brown (1995). HarperCollins.
Cats by Gail Gibbons (1996). Holiday House Books.
Click, Clack, Moo: Cows That Type by Doreen Cronin (2000). Simon & Schuster.
Curious George by H. A. Rey (1941). Houghton Mifflin Harcourt.
Ducks Don't Get Wet by Augusta R. Goldin (1965). Crowell.
Fish Eyes by Lois Ehlert (1992). Harcourt.
Five Little Pumpkins by Iris Van Rynbach (1995). Mills Press.
Frederick by Leo Lionni (1973). Dragonfly Books.
Giggle, Giggle, Quack by Doreen Cronin (2002). Atheneum Books.
Go Tell Aunt Rhody by Robert M. Quackenbush (1973). Lippincott Williams & Wilkins.
Knuffle Bunny by Mo Willems (2004). Hyperion Books.
Lilly's Purple Plastic Purse by Kevin Henkes (2006). Greenwillow Books.

The Milk Makers by Gail Gibbons (1987). Atheneum Books.

My Little Sister Ate One Hare by Bill Grossman (1998). Random House.

My, Oh My—A Butterfly! All About Butterflies by Tish Rabe (2007). Random House.

My Trip to the Farm by Mercer Mayer (2002). Dellosa.

The Napping House by Audrey Wood (2000). Houghton Mifflin Harcourt.

Old McDonald Had a Farm by Jane Cabrera (2008). Holiday House Books.

1, 2, 3 to the Zoo: A Counting Book by Eric Carle (1998). Philomel Books.

Over the River and Through the Wood by Lydia Maria Child (1999). North-South Books.

Raccoon on His Own by Jim Arnosky (2003). Puffin Books.

Spiders by Jane Resnick (1996). Kidsbooks.

Ten Dirty Pigs, Ten Clean Pigs by Carol Roth (2002). North-South.

Ten, nine, eight by Molly Bang (1991). HarperCollins.

The Very Busy Spider by Eric Carle (1985). Philomel Books.

The Very Hungry Caterpillar by Eric Carle (2007). Philomel Books.

Wee Sing, Animals, Animals, Animals by Pamela Conn Beall and Susan Hagen Nipp (2006). Price Stern Sloan.

IDEAS FOR DISCUSSION, REFLECTION, AND ACTION

1. At the beginning of the chapter there is an outline for a preschool day. Think about how you would organize the day differently. Prepare your day and be sure to include the literacy necessary for improved vocabulary and comprehension. When completed, evaluate what you wrote and in particular checking to see if you are providing the literacy instruction necessary.

2. This chapter describes units on animals and on seeds and planting. What other topics do you think are appropriate for preschool children? Try to think out of the box with topics. Select three topics and develop an activity for each that will engage the children in interesting projects.

3. Preschool teachers often don't get as much professional development as they should. If it isn't provided at your school, try setting your own goals for growth at the beginning of the school year. Locate books and articles on the areas you want to improve. Search for videos on a teaching channel. Look for conferences on the topic, and join a professional organization where you can learn from their conferences, journals, and members.

Selected Literature for the Preschool Classroom

Prepared by Kellyanne Healey

ALPHABET BOOKS

Bonder, D. (2007). *Dogabet*. North Vancouver, BC, Canada: Walrus.

Ernest, I. (2004). *The turn-around, upside down alphabet book*. New York: Simon & Schuster.

Fleming, D. (2006). *Alphabet under construction*. New York: Holt.

Lionni, L. (2004). *The alphabet tree*. New York: Random House.

Lluch, A. A. (2014). *Alphabet: I like to learn the ABC's*. San Diego, CA: WS Group.

Van Fleet, M. (2008). *Alphabet*. New York: Simon & Schuster.

NUMBER BOOKS

Blackstone, S. (2005). *My granny went to market: A round-the-world counting rhyme*. Cambridge, MA: Barefoot Books.

Carle, E. (1998). *1, 2, 3 to the zoo: A counting book*. New York: Putnam.

Crews, D. (1986). *Ten black dots*. New York: Greenwillow Books.

Jay, A. (2007). *1, 2, 3: A child's first counting book*. New York: Dutton.

Marsh, T. J. (1998). *Way out in the desert*. Flagstaff, AZ: Rising Moon.

McGinty, A. B. (2002). *Ten little lambs*. New York: Dial Books for Young Readers.

RHYMING BOOKS/NURSERY RHYMES

Brown, M. W. (2007). *Goodnight moon*. New York: HarperCollins.

Denton, K. (2004). *A child's treasury of nursery rhymes*. New York: Kingfisher.

Dr. Seuss. (1970). *Mr. Brown can moo! Can you?* New York: Random House.

Green, A. (2007). *Mother Goose's storytime nursery rhymes.* New York: Levine.
Grey, M. (2015). *The adventures of the dish and the spoon.* New York: Random House.
Mathers, P. (2012). *The McElderry book of Mother Goose: Revered and rare rhymes.* New York: McElderry.
Rescek, S. (2006). *Hickory, dickory dock: And other favorite nursery rhymes.* New York: Tiger Tales.

WORDLESS STORYBOOKS

Briggs, R. (1999). *The snowman.* New York: Random House.
dePaola, T. (1978). *Pancakes for breakfast.* Orlando, FL: Houghton Mifflin Harcourt.
Hutchins, P. (2005). *Rosie's walk.* New York: Simon & Schuster.
Mayer, M. (2003). *A boy, a dog, and a frog.* New York: Penguin Group.
Tafuri, N. (1991). *Have you seen my duckling?* New York: HarperCollins.

PREDICTABLE BOOKS

Adams, P. (2007). *There was an old lady who swallowed a fly.* Swindon, UK: Child's Play International.
Carle, E. (2001). *Today is Monday.* New York: Penguin.
Carle, E. (1967). *Brown bear, brown bear, what do you see?* New York: Holt.
Carle, E. (2007). *The very hungry caterpillar.* New York: Penguin.
Dean, J. (2013). *Pete the cat: The wheels on the bus.* New York: HarperCollins.

CULTURAL DIVERSITY

Adoff, A. (1973). *Black is brown is tan.* New York: HarperCollins.
Bunting, E. (2006). *One green apple.* New York: Clarion Books.
Dorros, A. (1993). *Radio man.* New York: Rayo.
Fox, M. (2006). *Whoever you are.* New York: Houghton Mifflin Harcourt.
Friedman, I. R. (1987). *How my parents learned to eat.* New York: Houghton Mifflin Harcourt.
Hoffman, M. (1991). *Amazing Grace.* New York: Dial Press.
Kissinger, K. (2002). *All the colors we are.* St. Paul, MN: Redleaf Press.

POETRY BOOKS

Brown, M. W. (2007). *Nibble nibble.* New York: HarperCollins.
Grimes, N. (2005). *It's raining laughter.* Honesdale, PA: Boyds Mills Press.
Heck, C. J. (2011). *Me too! Preschool poetry.* DuBois, PA: Barking Spiders.
Hoberman, M. A. (2006). *The llama who had no pajama.* New York: Harcourt.
Prelutsky, J. (2002). *The frogs who wore red suspenders.* New York: Harper-Trophy.

PICTURE BOOKS

Ahlberg, A. (2008). *The pencil.* Cambridge, MA: Candlewick.
Broach, E. (2007). *When dinosaurs came with everything.* New York: Atheneum.
Curtis, C. (2004). *I took the moon for a walk.* Cambridge, MA: Barefoot.
Fox, M. (2009). *The goblin and the empty chair.* New York: Beach Lane.
Hurd, T. (2010). *The weaver.* New York: Farrar Straus Giroux.
O'Callahan, J. (2009). *Raspberries!* New York: Philomel/Penguin.
Polacco, P. (2007). *Ginger and Petunia.* New York: Philomel/Penguin.
Yolen, J. (2009). *Come to the fairies' ball.* Honesdale, PA: Wordsong/Boyds Mills.

TRADITIONAL LITERATURE

Aylesworth, J. (2009). *The mitten.* New York: Scholastic.
Marshall, J. (1998). *Goldilocks and the three bears.* New York: Penguin.
Mosel, A. (2007). *Tikki tikki tembo.* New York: Square Fish.
Palatini, M. (2009). *Lousy rotten stinkin' grapes.* New York: Simon & Schuster.
Pinkney, J. (2000). *Aesop's fables.* San Francisco: Chronicle.
Pinkney, J. (2009). *The lion and the mouse.* New York: Little, Brown.
Spinner, S. (2008). *The nutcracker.* New York: Knopf.

BOOKS ABOUT FAMILY

Downey, R. (2001). *Love is a family.* New York: HarperCollins.
Eastman, P. D. (1998). *Are you my mother?* New York: Random House.

BOOKS FOR YOUNG READERS

Hausherr, R. (1997). *Celebrating families.* New York: Scholastic.
McCormick, W. (2002). *Daddy, will you miss me?* New York: Aladdin.
Parr, T. (2003). *The family book.* Boston: Little, Brown.
Williams, V. B. (1982). *A chair for my mother.* New York: Greenwillow.

INFORMATIONAL BOOKS

Jordan, D. (2012). *Dream big: Michael Jordan and the pursuit of Olympic gold.* New York: Simon & Schuster.
Razzak, S. (2007). *P is for Pakistan.* London: Lincoln.
Rubbino, S. (2009). *A walk in New York.* Cambridge, MA: Candlewick Press.
Showers, P. (1991). *How many teeth?* New York: HarperCollins.
Ziefert, H. (2006). *You can't taste a pickle with your ear!* Maplewood, NJ: Blue Apple.
Zoehfield, K. W. (1995). *What's alive?* New York: HarperCollins.

ANIMAL BOOKS

Aliki. (1999). *My visit to the zoo*. New York: HarperCollins.

Andreae, G., & Parker-Rees, G. (2001). *Giraffes can't dance*. London: Orchard.

Bancroft, H. (1997). *Animals in winter*. New York: HarperCollins.

Beall, P. C., & Nipp, S. H. (2006). *Wee sing, animals, animals, animals*. New York: Price Stern Sloan.

Campbell, R. (2007). *Dear zoo: A lift-the-flap book*. New York: Simon & Schuster.

Carle, E. (1977). *The grouchy ladybug*. New York: HarperCollins.

Carle, E. (1998). *1, 2, 3 to the zoo: A counting book*. New York: Putnam.

Chanko, P. (1998). *Baby animals learn*. New York: Scholastic.

Chessen, B., & Chanko, P. (1998). *Animal homes*. New York: Scholastic.

Jenkins, S. (2006). *Almost gone: The world's rarest animals* (Lets-Read-and-Find-Out series). New York: HarperCollins.

Keats, E. J. (1974). *Pet show*. New York: Aladdin.

Lauber, P., & Keller, H. (1995). *Who eats what? Food chains and food webs*. New York: HarperCollins.

Mora, P., & Cushman, D. (2006). *Marimba! Animales from A to Z*. New York: Houghton Mifflin.

Rabe, T. (2007). *My, oh my—a butterfly! All about butterflies* (Cat in the Hat's Learning Library). New York: Random House.

Relf, P., & Stevenson, N. (1995). *The magic school bus hops home: A book about animal habitats*. New York: Scholastic.

Satoh, A., & Toda, K. (1996). *Animal faces*. La Jolla, CA: Kane/Miller.

Staff of National Geographic, McKay, G., & McGhe, K. (2006). *National Geographic encyclopedia of animals*. Washington, DC: National Geographic Society.

Steig, W., & Puncel, M. (Trans.). (1997). *Doctor de soto* (Spanish ed.). New York: Farrar, Straus & Giroux.

Taylor, B. (1998). *A day at the farm*. New York: DK.

Wallace, K. (2003). *Trip to the zoo* (DK Readers series). New York: DK.

Yolen, J., & Teague, M. (2005). *How do dinosaurs eat their food?* New York: Harper & Row.

SCIENCE BOOKS

Barner, B. (1996). *Dem bones*. San Francisco: Chronicle.

Barner, B. (1999). *Bugs! Bugs! Bugs!*. San Francisco: Chronicle.

Cole, H. (1997). *Jack's garden*. New York: Greenwillow.

Ehlert, L. (1992). *Planting a rainbow*. New York: Houghton Mifflin Harcourt.

Martin, B. (2011). *Ten little caterpillars*. New York: Beach Lane.

BOOKS ABOUT THE WEATHER

Barrett, J. (1982). *Cloudy with a chance of meatballs*. New York: Atheneum.

Burke, J. S. (2000). *Cold days*. New York: Welcome.

Burke, J. S. (2000). *Hot days*. New York: Welcome.

dePaola, T. (1984). *The cloud book*. New York: Holiday House.

Inkpen, M. (2001). *Kipper's rainy day*. New York: Red Wagon.

Inkpen, M. (2001). *Kipper's sunny day*. New York: Red Wagon.

E-Book Quality Rating Tool

E-book title: _____

Source: _____

Rater: _____

Date: _____

This tool has three general categories for rating the quality of an e-book: (1) ease of use (easy for child to pick and use), (2) multimedia (use of auditory, visual, and touch media), and (3) interaction (multimodal: seeing, hearing, touching). Each category has several features. Each feature has a criterion to judge quality. Rate the extent to which the criterion is met for each feature. Keep in mind that not every book has every feature and the more features does not mean higher quality.

Key: LE = large extent, equals 1 point; SE = some extent, equals 0.5 point; NE = no extent, equals 0 points; NA means "not applicable" and is not computed. To obtain a score, add up the points and divide by the number of items. Total points = 20.

From Roskos, Brueck, and O'Brien (2011). Reprinted with permission from the authors.

Category	Feature	Criterion	Rating			
			NA	LE	SE	NE
Ease of use (8)	Home page	Access is quick; easy				
	Start/stop/pause buttons	Large; easy to select				
	Previous/next buttons	Large; easy to select				
	Manual/auto control buttons	Easy to locate and select				
	Separate modes (e.g., with/ without narration)	Easy to switch between modes				
	Page numbers	Present; easy to see on screen				
	Child control and mastery	In child's motor skill range; supports independence; responsive to child actions				
	User guidance	Directions easy to follow; given verbally; accompanied by pictures				
Multimedia (8)	Print font size	Sufficiently large; age appropriate				
	Amount of text per screen	Age appropriate; avoids information overload				
	Print highlights	Synced with the narration at paragraph, sentence, or word level				
	Print–graphics match	Meaningful; supportive of story comprehension				
	Music effects	Meaningful to book content; motivating; not distracting				
	Audio narration	Appealing to young children; well paced				
	Animations	Meaningful to story comprehension; motivating				
	Sound effects	Meaningful; appealing to children; not distracting				

(continued)

Category	Feature	Criterion	Rating			
			NA	LE	SE	NE
Interaction (4)	With text (sentences, words, letters)	Dictionary option with pictures, animations, or oral explanations				
	With educational content	Disciplinary content in one or more areas, including vocabulary				
	With illustrations	Active illustration option with auditory or visual options to encourage exploration (hot spots)				
	With games	In a separate mode; connected to theme or topic				
Rate the e-book						
1 = low; 20 = high						

— — — — — — — — — — — — — — — — — — —

1 2 3 4 5 6 7 8 9 10 11 12 13 14 15 16 17 18 19 20

Storytelling Ideas
for Developing Comprehension

This appendix contains stories that emphasize specific storytelling techniques for teachers to use with their children: sound story, chalk talk, origami story, and prop story.

SOUND STORY

Sample Story: "The Grouchy Queen and the Happy King"
(Adapted from an Anonymous Tale)

When the underlined words are mentioned, the following sounds are made:

> <u>Queen Grace the Grouch</u>: *Grrrrr.*
> <u>King Happy Herman</u>: *Ha-ha-ha.*
> <u>Whistling Wilbur</u>: *Whistling sound high to low.*
> <u>Singing Sam</u>: *La-la-la (first few notes of "Mary Had a Little Lamb").*
> <u>Tired Tim</u>: *Ahhhh (yawning sound).*
> <u>Lively Lorraine</u>: *Ah ha.*

Once upon a time there was a queen named <u>Grace the Grouch</u>. She had this name because she growled most of the time. <u>Queen Grace the Grouch</u> was married to <u>King Happy Herman</u>. He was called <u>Happy Herman</u> because he laughed most of the time. Together they made a perfect couple. <u>Queen Grace the Grouch</u> and <u>King Happy Herman</u> had three sons. The first son's name was <u>Whistling Wilbur</u>. He had this name because he whistled almost all the time. The second son's name was <u>Singing Sam</u>. He had this name because most of the time he sang. The third son's name was <u>Tired Tim</u>. He had this name because most of the time he was sleeping, and when he was awake he was doing almost nothing but yawning.

There was a princess from the next kingdom named <u>Lively Lorraine</u>. She couldn't sit still for a moment. She bounced around from dawn till dusk looking for things to do. Each time the princess would find a job to be done, she'd lift her hand in the air and say, "Ah ha." When most people spoke of Lorraine, they could not help but say, "Ah ha."

Lively Lorraine decided that she'd like to marry. She knew of Queen Grace the Grouch and her husband, King Happy Herman. She also knew about their three sons, Whistling Wilbur, Singing Sam, and Tired Tim. Lively Lorraine decided to take a look at the three princes to see if one might be a suitable future king for her. She saddled her horse one day and away she galloped to the kingdom over the hill.

When she arrived, she was greeted by Queen Grace the Grouch and her husband, King Happy Herman. Lively Lorraine decided to stay a while to get to know each prince and to see if there was one that best suited her.

First, Lively Lorraine played tennis with Whistling Wilbur. But he whistled so much throughout the game that Lively Lorraine could not concentrate and kept missing the ball.

The next day, Lorraine went sailing with Singing Sam. Sam was nice, but he never stopped singing. Instead of talking, he'd find an appropriate song and sing what he had to say. For a while it was fun, but Lorraine tired of it quickly.

Lively Lorraine felt sad. She decided that she would not meet the prince of her dreams here in this kingdom. But suddenly, Tired Tim came yawning down the garden path. Lorraine took one look at him and said, "Ah ha." Somehow Lively Lorraine and Tired Tim made the perfect couple—something like Queen Grace the Grouch and King Happy Herman.

So Lively Lorraine and Tired Tim trotted off to the kingdom over the hill to be married. Of course, they lived happily ever after.

CHALK TALK

Sample Story: "The Surprise in the Playhouse" (Adapted from an Anonymous Tale)

In this story, the underlined words indicate when to draw.

There was once a little girl named Lori, and there is an L for Lori. Lori found a great big empty refrigerator box one day outside a neighbor's house; it was left for the garbage man to pick up.

Lori decided that the refrigerator box would make a terrific playhouse. She dragged the box home and set it in her backyard, and it looked like this.

The house needed a lot of work. The first thing Lori did was to cut out two squares to make windows, like this. Then she drew some pretty shutters that looked like these.

When she finished with the windows, she cut out a door just like this.

Lori wanted a way to get in and out of her house from the back. She thought about it a while and decided to make the back all open so it would feel bigger inside and a lot of light could shine in. To do this, she cut the sides of the box, on both sides, down the middle, and pulled the flaps open. It made the house look like this.

Lori found some tiny garden fencing in her garage. She put the fence in front of her playhouse and planted seeds behind the fence.

Now that her house was finished, she thought she'd go get her friend Linda. That's another <u>L</u> for Linda.

Linda lived across the street and down the block. So Lori skipped <u>across the street and went down the block</u> to Linda's house. <u>She went to the front door</u> and rang the bell.

Linda's mother came to the door and said that Linda was upstairs in her room playing. So <u>Lori went upstairs</u> and asked Linda if she would like to see her new playhouse.

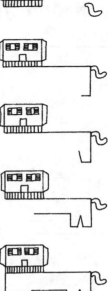

Linda said yes, so <u>the two girls hurried down the stairs</u>. Linda forgot her sweater so <u>she ran back up again</u> to get it. Now the girls were ready to go. <u>They went across the street</u> and were on their way back to Lori's house.

Lori stopped a minute and <u>bent down to look</u> at a caterpillar. Linda looked, too. <u>The girls got up and hurried along</u>. Then they pretended they were bunnies and <u>jumped up and down as they went</u>. <u>Lori fell down and Linda helped her up.</u>

ORIGAMI STORY

Sample Story: Swimmy by Leo Lionni (2005)

A little black fish escapes being eaten by a giant tuna and finds comfort and safety in numbers with his new friends. Origami technique: Fold paper into the shape of a fish.

Activity

1. Practice folding origami figures until you feel confident with the technique and can fold and tell the story smoothly.
2. While telling the story, fold the paper into the main character or object and display it until the story is ended.

Origami Fish

Enlarge as needed. Fold as indicated in order by number.

PROP STORY

Sample Story: "The Little Round Red House"

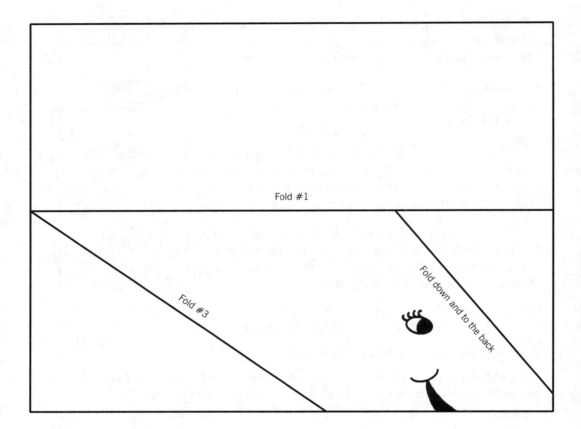

Fold #1

Fold #3

Fold down and to the back

(Adapted from an Anonymous Tale)

School had ended for the summer. Stephanie was wandering around the house trying to find something to do. She colored for a while, cut and pasted, and looked at some books, but nothing seemed like much fun. She looked for her mother. Her mother was at her desk, busy with some important work.

Stephanie said to her mother, "What can I do today? I just can't seem to find anything."

Her mother thought for a while and said, "Stephanie, I know what you can do. Go outside for a walk and see if you can find a little round red house that has no windows and no doors, a chimney on top, and a star inside."

Stephanie wasn't really sure what her mother was talking about, but since it sounded interesting she decided to give it a try. First, Stephanie walked down Elm Street. Then she tried Heritage Lane, but not one house fit the description her mother had given.

She could not find a little round red house that had no windows and no doors, a chimney on top, and a star inside. All the houses had windows and doors. None of the houses was even red.

When she was about to give up and go home, she met her friend Darren. He was looking for something to do. Stephanie asked him to help her with her search. The two children decided to ask Mr. and Mrs. Mandel if they knew of this little round red house. Mr. and Mrs. Mandel owned the candy shop, and they knew everything about the town in which Stephanie and Darren lived. If anyone would know about such a strange house, it would be the Mandels.

Stephanie ran into the candy shop. She immediately asked Mrs. Mandel if she knew of a little round red house that had no windows and no doors, a chimney on top, and a star inside. Mrs. Mandel thought for a while and then said, "Stephanie, go down to the shady pond where the wind blows through the trees. Sit down a while to enjoy the summer day and the breeze rippling through the trees, and maybe you will find what you are looking for."

Darren and Stephanie hurried down to the shady pond. It was a long walk and the day was hot, so they were happy to sit down and rest by the pond in the shade of the trees. Before long, a lovely cool breeze blew through the branches of the trees. The leaves rustled, and something fell out of one of the trees.

Whatever fell bounced first on Stephanie's head and then fell to the ground. It had split into two pieces. Stephanie picked up the two pieces and put them back together again. Then she began to laugh. "My goodness," she said, "I've found it! This is the little round red house that has no windows and no doors, a chimney on top, and a star inside." Hungry from their experience, Darren and Stephanie each took a piece and enjoyed the apple [show cut apple] that had fallen from the tree.

Cut apple on the dotted line.

Guided Participation Framework

Step 1: Get ready.

_____ Have materials out.

_____ Sit near the children.

_____ Get their attention.

_____ Name what you will do.

_____ Ask them to join in.

Step 2: Build meaning.

_____ Help children join in.

_____ Show them how.

_____ Ask them to check their thinking.

_____ Talk about what you are doing.

_____ Help them succeed.

Step 3: Make connections.

_____ Help children think about the activity.

_____ Help them remember past experiences like it.

_____ Ask them to predict what they will do.

_____ Help them anticipate actions.

_____ Encourage their ideas.

Step 4: Have fun.

_____ Smile at the children.

_____ Respond to their words and actions.

_____ Show you care.

_____ Laugh with them.

_____ Enjoy the time spent.

Recommended Resources
for New and Alternative Literacies

WEBSITES

McGraw-Hill Website for Children's Literature

www.mhhe.com/socscience/education/kidlit

A database of children's literature, online lesson plans, and activities to implement in the classroom, as well as featured authors and books of the month.

Preschool at the Literacy Web

www.literacy.uconn.edu/pkhome.htm

A literacy web resource page that includes easy access to a wide assortment of literacy ideas customized for use by preschoolers and their teachers.

TogetheREAD

www.togetheread.com

A resource page that includes recommended books and activities to promote family literacy.

Books and Literature Preschool Activities and Crafts

www.first-school.ws/theme/books.htm

Activities and art projects to reinforce comprehension of children's literature in preschool classrooms.

International Children's Digital Library

www.icdlbooks.org

An international children's digital library meant to excite and inspire the world's children to become members of the global community by making the best in children's literature available online.

PBS Kids' Stories

www.pbskids.org/clifford/stories/index.html

Clifford the Big Red Dog online stories, plus accompanying worksheets, coloring, and games.

Reading Is Fundamental

www.rif.org/kids/leadingtoreading/en/preschoolers/read.htm

This site features online stories and also includes sing-alongs, games, and other resources for parents.

TELEVISION SHOWS BASED ON CHILDREN'S LITERATURE

Arthur

This story is about an aardvark and his interactions with peers and family. The series often deals with social and health-related issues that affect young children. There is also a strong emphasis on the educational value of books and libraries.

Clifford the Big Red Dog

The runt of the litter, Clifford was chosen by a city child named Emily Elizabeth Howard as her birthday present. Clifford grew to over 25 feet tall, forcing the family to leave the city and move to an open suburb.

Berenstain Bears

A family of bears living in Bear Country deals with topics relevant to family life.

Curious George

A curious chimpanzee named George leaves his home in Africa to live with "the man with the yellow hat" in a big city. An animated television series was developed from the book's plot and characters.

Winnie the Pooh

The lovable bear Winnie the Pooh and his master, Christopher Robin, and friends have many fun adventures taking place in the Hundred Acre Wood. The show brings alive the humor and excitement of the original books.

Little Bear

Little Bear is a grizzly bear cub, who gets into trouble and has wonderful adventures with his other animal friends. The show teaches children about emotions and feelings, and how to deal with them as shown through the relatable characters.

The Magic School Bus

Ms. Frizzle and her class board a magical school bus that takes them on field trips to places of great imagination. This bus can also transform into a spaceship, a boat, and an animal. The show aims to teach children about science through an interactive approach.

Ella the Elephant

Ella is a spirited elephant with a great imagination, a big heart, and a magic hat that can transform into almost anything. The series follows Ella and her friends on their adventures on Elephant Island.

References

Applebee, A. N., Langer, J. A., & Mullis, M. (1988). *Who reads best?: Factors related to reading achievement in 3, 7, and 11*. Princeton, NJ: Educational Testing Service.

Baumann, J. F., Seifert-Kessell, N., & Jones, L. A. (1992). Effect of think-aloud instruction on elementary students' comprehension monitoring abilities. *Journal of Reading Behavior, 24*(2), 143–172.

Beck, I. L., McKeown, M. G., & Kucan, L. (2013). *Bringing words to life: Robust vocabulary instruction* (2nd ed.). New York: Guilford Press.

Biemiller, A. (2006). Vocabulary development and instruction: A prerequisite for school learning. In D. K. Dickinson & S. B. Neuman (Eds.), *Handbook of early literacy research* (Vol. 2, pp. 41–51). New York: Guilford Press.

Biemiller, A. (2010). *Words worth teaching: Closing the vocabulary gap*. Columbus, OH: McGraw-Hill.

Biemiller, A., & Boote, C. (2006). An effective method for building meaning vocabulary in primary grades. *Journal of Educational Psychology, 98*(1), 44.

Biemiller, A., & Slonim, N. (2001). Estimating root word vocabulary growth in normative and advantaged populations: Evidence for a common sequence of vocabulary acquisition. *Journal of Education and Psychology, 93*(3), 498–520.

Blair, C. (2002). School readiness: Integrating cognition and emotion in a neurobiological conceptualization of children's functioning at school entry. *American Psychologist, 57*(2), 111–127.

Bloom, P. (2002). Mindreading, communicate, and the learning of the names for things. *Mind and Language, 17*(1, 2), 37–54.

Bodrova, E., & Leong, D. J. (2007). *Tools of the mind: The Vygotskian approach to early childhood education* (2nd ed.). Columbus, OH: Merrill/Prentice Hall.

Bouffard, S., Westmoreland, H., O'Carroll, K., & Little, P. (2011). *Promising practices for family engagement in out-of-school time*. Charlotte, NC: Information Age.

Bowman, B. T., Donovan, S., & Burns, M. S. (2001). *Eager to learn: Educating our preschoolers*. Washington, DC: National Academies Press.

Breneman, L., & Breneman, B. (1983). *Once upon a time: A storytelling handbook.* Chicago: Nelson-Hall.

Bruner, J. (1983). *Child's talk: Learning to use language.* New York: Norton.

Burns, M. S., Snow, C. E., & Griffin, P. (Eds.). (1999). *Starting out right: A guide to promoting children's reading success.* Washington, DC: National Academies Press.

Burstein, K., & Roskos, K. (2011, April). *Design considerations for an effective ebook physical environment.* Paper presented at the annual meeting of the American Educational Research Association, New Orleans, LA.

Bus, A. G., & Both-de Vries, A. C. (2008, March). *Name writing as a catalyst for phonenc awareness.* Paper presented at the annual meeting of the American Educational Research Association, New York.

Bus, A. G., van IJzendoorn, M. H., & Pellegrini, A. D. (1995). Joint book reading makes for success in learning to read: A meta-analysis on intergenerational transmission of literacy. *Review of Educational Research, 65*(1), 1–21.

Charters, J., & Gately, A. (1986). *Drama anytime.* Portsmouth, NH: Heinemann Educational Books.

Christie, J., Enz, B., & Vukelich, C. (2007). *Teaching language and literacy: Preschool through the elementary grades* (3rd ed.). New York: Allyn & Bacon.

Cochran-Smith, M. (1984). *The making of a reader.* Norwood, NH: Ablex.

Cullinan, B. E. (1992). *Invitation to read: More children's literature in the reading program.* Newark, DE: International Reading Association.

Cunningham, A. E., & Zibulsky, J. (2014). *Book smart: How to develop and support successful, motivated readers.* Oxford, UK: Oxford University Press.

Dangel, J. R., & Durden, T. R. (2010). The nature of teacher talk during small group activities. *Young Children,* 74–81.

Diamond, A., Barnett, W. S., Thomas, J., & Munro, S. (2007). Preschool program improves cognitive control. *Science, 318*(5855), 1387–1388.

Dickinson, D. K., McCabe, A., & Sprague, K. (2003). Teacher Rating of Oral Language and Literacy (TROLL): Individualizing early literacy instruction with a standards-based rating tool. *The Reading Teacher, 56*(6), 554–564.

Dickinson, D. K., & Neuman, S. B. (Eds.). (2006). *Handbook of early literacy research* (Vol. 2). New York: Guilford Press.

Dickinson, D. K., & Tabors, P. O. (Eds.). (2001). *Beginning literacy with language.* Baltimore, MD: Brookes.

Dixon, L. Q., Zhao, J., Shin, J. Y., Wu, S., Su, J. H., Burgess-Brigham, R., et al. (2012). What we know about second language acquisition: A synthesis from four perspectives. *Review of Educational Research, 82*(1), 5–60.

Dorr, R. E. (2006). Something old is new again: Revisiting language experience. *The Reading Teacher, 60*(2), 138–146.

Dougherty, C. (2014). Starting off strong: The importance of early learning. *American Educator, 38*(2), 14–18.

Duke, N. K. (2004). The case for informational text. *Educational Leadership, 61*(6), 40–44.

Dunn, L. M., & Dunn, D. M. (2007). *Peabody Picture Vocabulary Test—Fourth Edition.* Bloomington, MN: NCS Pearson.

Edwards, P. (1995). Combining parents' and teachers' thoughts about storybook reading at home and school. In L. M. Morrow (Ed.), *Family literacy connections in schools and communities* (pp. 54–69). Newark, DE: International Reading Association.

Ehri, L. (2014). Orthographic mapping in the acquisition of sight word reading, spelling memory, and vocabulary learning, *Scientific Studies of Reading, 18*(1), 5–21.

Ehri, L., & Roberts, T. (2006). The roots of learning to read and write: Acquisition of letters and phonemic awareness. *Handbook of Early Literacy Research, 2,* 113–131.

Essa, E. L., & Burnham, M. M. (Eds.). (2009). *Informing our practice: Useful research on young children's development.* Washington, DC: National Association for the Education of Young Children.

Fernald, A., & Weisleder, A. (2011). *How and why early experience is so crucial in learning language.* Paper presented at the LENA Users Conference, Denver, CO.

Fountas, I. C., & Pinnell, G. S. (1996). *Guided reading: Good first teaching for all children.* Portsmouth, NH: Heinemann.

Gambrell, L. B. (2009). Creating opportunities to read more so that our students read better. In E. H. Hiebert (Ed.), *Reading more, reading better* (pp. 251–266). New York: Guilford Press.

Gambrell, L. B., Pfeiffer, W., & Wilson, R. (1985). The effects of retelling upon reading comprehension and recall of text information. *Journal of Educational Research, 78,* 216–220.

Gillam, S., & Reutzel, D. R. (2013). Speaking and listening standards. In L. M. Morrow, T. Shanahan, & K. Wixson (Eds.), *Teaching with the Common Core State Standards for English language arts: PreK–2* (pp. 107–127). New York: Guilford Press.

Goldenberg, C. (2008). Teaching English language learners. *American Educator,* 8–23, 43–44.

Graves, M. F. (2010). *Teaching reading in the 21st century.* Boston: Allyn & Bacon.

Guthrie, J. T. (2002). Engagement and motivation in reading instruction. In L. Kamil, J. B. Manning, & H. J. Wallberg (Eds.), *Successful reading instruction* (pp. 137–154). Greenwich, CT: Information Age.

Hannon, P. (1995). *Literacy, home, and school: Research and practice in teaching literacy with parents.* London: Falmer Press.

Harris, J., Golinkoff, R. M., & Hirsh-Pasek, K. (2011). Lessons from the crib for the classroom: How children really learn vocabulary. In S. B. Neuman & D. K. Dickinson (Eds.), *Handbook of early literacy research* (Vol. 3, pp. 49–65). New York: Guilford Press.

Hart, B., & Risley, T. (1995). *Meaningful differences in the everyday experiences of young American children.* Baltimore, MD: Brookes.

Hart, B., & Risley, T. (2003). The early catastrophe: The 30 million word gap. *American Educator, 27*(1), 4–9.

Hawley, W., & Valli, L. (1999). The essentials of effective professional development: A new consensus. In L. Darling-Hammond & G. Sykes (Eds.), *Teaching as the learning profession: Handbook of policy and practice* (pp. 127–150). San Franciso: Jossey-Bass.

Head Start Child and Learning Development Framework. (2010). Retrieved from *https://eclkc.ohs.acf.hhs.gov/hslc/tta-system/teaching/eecd/Assessment/Child%20Outcomes/HS_Revised_Child_Outcomes_Framework(rev-Sept2011).pdf.*

Heath, S. N. (1982). What no bedtime story means. *Language in Society, 11,* 49–76.

Hindman, A. H., & Wasik, B. A. (2012). Morning message time: An exploratory study in Head Start. *Early Childhood Education, 40,* 275–283.

Hirsch, E. (2006). Building knowledge. *American Educator, 30*(1), 8–51.

Holdaway, D. (1979). *The foundations of literacy.* Sydney, Australia: Ashton Scholastic.

Holdaway, D., & University of Western Ontario Faculty of Education. (1984). *Stability and change in literacy learning.* Portsmouth, NH: Heinemann.

Huck, C. (1992). Literacy and literature. *Language Arts, 69,* 520–526.

Johnson, J. E., Christie, J. F., & Wardle, F. (2005). *Play, development, and early education.* Boston: Allyn & Bacon.

Kreider, H., & Westmoreland, H. (2011). *Promising practices for family engagement in out-of-school time.* Charlotte, NC: Information Age.

Lackney, J. A. (2003). *33 principles of educational design.* School Design Research Studio. Retrieved August 2006, from *http://school studio. engr.wisc.edu/33principles.html.*

Leichter, H. J. (1984). Families as an environment for literacy. In H. Goelman, A. A. Oberg, & F. Smith (Eds.), *Awakening to literacy* (pp. 38–50). Portsmouth, NH: Heineman.

Lobman, C., & O'Neill, B. E. (2011). *Play and performance: Play and culture studies.* Lanham, MD: University Press of America.

Lombardino, L. J., Lieberman, R. J., & Brown, J. J. C. (2009) *ALL: Assessment of literacy and language.* Boston: Pearson Education.

Lonigan, C. J., & Whitehurst, G. J. (1998). Relative efficacy of parent and teacher involvement in a shared-reading intervention for preschool children from low-income backgrounds. *Early Childhood Research Quarterly, 13*(2), 263–290.

Manning, M., Manning, G., & Long, R. (1994). *Theme immersion: Inquiry-based curriculum in elementary and middle schools.* Portsmouth, NH: Heinemann.

Mardell, B. (1999). *From basketball to the Beatles: In search of compelling early childhood curriculum.* Portsmith, NH: Heinemann.

Marulis, L., & Neuman, S. B. (2010). The effects of vocabulary intervention on young children's word learning: A meta-analysis. *Review of Educational Research, 80*(3), 300–335.

McGee, L. M., & Richgels, D. J. (2012). *Literacy's beginnings: Supporting young readers and writers.* Boston: Pearson.

McGraw-Hill/Wright Group. (2002). *Doors to discovery assessment handbook.* Columbus, OH: McGraw-Hill Education.

McKenna, M. C. (2001). Development of reading attitudes. In L. Verhoeven & C. Snow (Eds.), *Literacy and motivation: Reading engagement in individuals and groups* (pp. 135–158). Mahwah, NJ: Erlbaum.

Morrow, L. M. (1984). Reading stories to young children: Effects of story structure and traditional questioning strategies on comprehension. *Journal of Reading Behavior, 16,* 273–288.

Morrow, L. M. (1985). Retelling stories: A strategy for improving young children's comprehension, concept of story structure, and oral language complexity. *Elementary School Journal, 85*(3), 646–661.

Morrow, L. M. (1986). *Promoting responses to literature: Children's sense of story structure.* Paper presented at the National Reading Conference, Austin, TX.

Morrow, L. M. (1987). Promoting voluntary reading: The effects of an inner city program in summer day care centers. *The Reading Teacher, 41,* 266–274.

Morrow, L. M. (1988a). Retelling stories as a diagnostic tool. In S. M. Glazer, L. W. Searfoss, & L. M. Gentile (Eds.), *Reexamining reading diagnosis: New trends and procedures* (pp. 128–149). Newark, DE: International Reading Association.

Morrow, L. M. (1988b). Young children's responses to one-to-one story reading in school settings. *Reading Research Quarterly, 5,* 537–554.

Morrow, L. M. (1990). Preparing the classroom environment to promote literacy during play. *Early Childhood Research Quarterly, 5*(4), 537–554.

Morrow, L. M. (1992). The impact of a literature-based program on literacy achievement, use of literature, and attitudes of children from minority backgrounds. *Reading Research Quarterly, 27*(3), 250–275.

Morrow, L. M. (1996). Story retelling: A discussion strategy to develop and assess comprehension. In L. B. Gambrell & J. F. Almasi (Eds.), *Lively discussion: Fostering engaged reading* (pp. 265–285). Newark, DE: International Reading Association.

Morrow, L. M. (2002). *The literacy center: Contexts for reading and writing* (2nd ed.). York, ME: Stenhouse.

Morrow, L. M. (2005). Language and literacy in preschools: Current issues and concerns. *Literacy Teaching and Learning, 9*(1), 7–19.

Morrow, L. M. (2014). *Literacy development in the early years* (8th ed.). Boston: Pearson.

Morrow, L. M. (2015). *Literacy development in the early years: Helping children read and write* (8th ed.). Upper Saddle River, NJ: Pearson.

Morrow, L. M., O'Connor, E. M., & Smith, J. (1990). Effects of a story reading program on the literacy development of at-risk kindergarten children. *Journal of Reading Behavior, 20*(20), 140–141.

Moss, B., Leone, S., & Dipillo, M. L. (1997). Exploring the literature of fact: Linking reading and writing through information trade books. *Language Arts, 74*(6), 418–429.

Nagy, W. (1988). *Teaching vocabulary to improve reading comprehension.* Newark, DE: International Reading Association.

National Early Literacy Panel. (2008). Developing early literacy: A scientific synthesis of early literacy development and implications for intervention. Retrieved April 8, 2009, from *www.nifl.gov/publications/pdf/NELPReport09.pdf.*

National Governors Association for Best Practices & Council of Chief State School Officers. (2010). *Common Core State Standards for English language arts and literacy in history/social studies, science, and technical subjects.* Washington, DC: Author. Available at *www.corestandards.org.*

National Institute of Child Health and Human Development. (2000). *Report of the National Reading Panel: Teaching children to read: An evidence-based assessment of the scientific research literature on reading and its implications for reading instruction* (NIH Publication No. 00-4769). Washington, DC: U.S. Government Printing Office.

Neuman, S. B., & Roskos, K. A. (1989). Preschoolers' conceptions of literacy as reflected in their spontaneous play. In S. McCormick, J. Zutell, P. Scharer, & P. R. O'Keefe (Eds.), *Cognitive and social perspective for literacy research and instruction* (38th yearbook of the National Reading Conference, pp. 87–94). Chicago: National Reading Conference.

Neuman, S. [B.], & Roskos, K. A. (1997). Literacy knowledge in practice: Contexts of participation for young writers and readers. *Reading Research Quarterly, 32,* 10–32.

Neuman, S. B., & Roskos, K. A. (2007). *Nurturing knowledge: Building a foundation for school success by linking early literacy to math, science, art and social studies.* New York: Scholastic.

Neuman, S. B., & Wright, T. (2014). The magic of words: Teaching vocabulary in the early childhood classroom. *American Educator, 38*(2), 4–14.

New Standards Speaking and Listening Committee. (2001). *Speaking and listening for preschool through third grade.* Washington, DC: National Center on Education and the Economy and University of Pittsburgh.

Ninio, A. (1980). Picture book reading in mother–infant dyads belonging to two subgroups in Israel. *Child Development, 51,* 587.

Ogle, D. (1986). K-W-L: A teaching model that develops active reading of expository text. *The Reading Teacher, 39,* 564–570.

Pearson, P. D., Roehler, L. R., Dole, J. A., & Duffy, G. G. (1992). Developing expertise in reading comprehension. In S. J. Samuels & A. E. Farsturp (Eds.), *What research has to say about reading instruction* (2nd ed., pp. 145–199). Newark, DE: International Reading Association.

Pellegrini, A., & Galda, L. (1982). The effects of thematic fantasy play training on the development of children's story comprehension. *American Educational Research Journal, 19,* 443–452.

Perfetti, C., & Stafura, J. (2014). Word knowledge in a theory of reading comprehension. *Scientific Studies of Reading, 18,* 22–37.

Pianta, R., La Paro, K., & Hamre, B. K. (2008). *Classroom assessment scoring system.* Baltimore, MD: Brookes.

Pressley, M., & Hilden, K. (2002). How can children be taught to comprehend text better? In M. L. Kamil, J. B. Manning, & H. J. Walberg (Eds.), *Successful reading instruction* (pp. 33–53). Greenwich, CT: Information Age.

RAND Reading Study Group. (2002). *Reading for understanding: Toward a research and development program in reading comprehension.* Santa Monica, CA: Office of Education Research and Improvement.

Ritchie, S., James-Szanton, J., & Howes, C. (2002). Emergent literacy practices in early childhood classrooms. In C. Howes (Ed.), *Teaching 4- to 8-year-olds: Literacy, math, multiculturalism, and classroom community* (pp. 71–92). Baltimore, MD: Brookes.

Robbins, C., & Ehri, L. C. (1994). Reading storybooks to kindergartners helps them learn new vocabulary words. *Journal of Educational Psychology, 86*(1), 54–64.

Roser, N., & Martinez, M. (1985). Roles adults play in preschool responses to literatures. *Language Arts, 62,* 485–490.

Roskos, K. A. (2008). *Language for learning in the early years.* Akron, OH: University of Akron Center for Literacy. Retrieved from *http://prod.ereadohio.org/ode/llo.*

Roskos, K. [A.], Brueck, J., & O'Brien, C. (2011). *Technical Report No. 1: Developing an ebook quality rating tool.* Paper presented at the annual meeting of the American Educational Research Association, New Orleans, LA.

Roskos, K. [A.], & Christie, J. F. (2007). *Play and literacy in early childhood: Research from multiple perspectives* (2nd ed.). New York: Erlbaum.

Roskos, K. [A.], & Christie, J. [F.] (2013). Strengthening play in early literacy teaching practice. In D. Barone & M. Mallette (Eds.), *Best practices in early literacy instruction* (pp. 251–268). New York: Guilford Press.

Roskos, K. A., Lenhart, L. A., & Noll, B. L. (2012). *Early Literacy Materials Selector (ELMS): A tool for review of early literacy program materials*. Thousand Oaks: Corwin Press.

Roskos, K. A., Tabors, P., & Lenhart, L. (2009). *Oral language and early literacy in preschool: Talking, reading, and writing*. Newark, DE: International Reading Association.

Samuels, S. J. (1987). Factors that influence listening and reading comprehension. In R. Horowitz & S. Jay Samuels (Eds.), *Comprehending oral and written language* (pp. 295–325). New York: Academic Press.

Saville-Troike, M. (1987). Bilingual discourse: The negotiation of meaning without a common code. *Linguistics, 25*, 81–106.

Scarborough, H. S. (2001). Connecting early language and literacy to later reading (dis)abilities: Evidence, theory, and practice. In S. B. Neuman & D. K. Dickinson (Eds.), *Handbook of early literacy research* (Vol. 1, pp. 97–110). New York: Guilford Press.

Sénéchal, M. (1997). The differential effect of storybook reading on preschoolers' acquisition of expressive and receptive vocabulary. *Child Language, 24*, 123–138.

Sénéchal, M., & Cornell, E. H. (1993). Vocabulary acquisition through shared reading experiences. *Reading Research Quarterly, 28*, 360–374.

Silverman, R. (2007). A comparison of three methods of vocabulary instruction during read-alouds in kindergarten. *Elementary School Journal, 108*(2), 97–113.

Singer, D. G., & Singer, J. L. (1990). *The house of make believe: Children's play and the developing imagination*. Cambridge, MA: Harvard University Press.

Smeets, D. J., & Bus, A. G. (2012). Interactive electronic storybooks for kindergartners to promote vocabulary growth. *Journal of Experimental Child Psychology, 112*(1), 36–55.

Smith, P. K. (2007). Pretend play and children's cognitive and literacy development: Sources of evidence and some lessons from the past. In K. A. Roskos & J. F. Christie (Eds.), *Play and literacy in early childhood: Research from multiple perspectives* (pp. 3–20). Mahwah, NJ: Erlbaum.

Snow, C. E., Burns, M. S., & Griffin, P. (Eds.). (1998). *Preventing reading difficulties in young children*. Washington, DC: National Academies Press.

Soderman, A. K., Gregory, K. M., & O'Neill, L. T. (1999). *Scaffolding emergent literacy: A child-centered approach for preschool through grade 5*. Columbus, OH: Merrill.

Stanovich, K. E. (1986). Matthew effects in reading: Some consequences of individual differences in the acquisition of literacy. *Reading Research Quarterly, 21*(4), 360–407.

Stauffer, R. G. (1980). *The language-experience approach to the teaching of reading* (2nd ed.). New York: Harper & Row.

Sulzby, E., & Teale, W. (1987). *Young children's storybook reading: Longitudinal study of parent–child interaction and children's independent functioning*. Final report to the Spencer Foundation, University of Michigan, Ann Arbor.

Tabors, P. O. (2008). *One child, two languages: A guide for early childhood educators of children learning English as a second language* (2nd ed.). Baltimore, MD: Brookes.

Taylor, D., & Strickland, D. S. (1986). *Family storybook reading*. Portsmouth, NH: Heinemann.

Teale, W. H. (1981). Parents reading to their children: What we know and need to know. *Language Arts, 58*, 902–912.

Test, J. E., Cunningham, D. D., & Lee, A. C. (2010). Talking with young children: How teachers encourage learning. *Dimensions of Early Childhood, 38*(3), 3–13

Tough, J. (1981). *A place for talk: The role of talk in the education of the children with moderate learning difficulties.* London: Ward Lock Educational.

Umek, L. M., & Peklaj, U. F. (2010). The role of symbolic play in early literacy development. *Journal of Communications Research, 1*(4), 291–308.

Vukelich, C., Evans, C., & Albertson, B. (2003). Organizing expository texts: A look at the possibilities. In D. M. Barone & L. M. Morrow (Eds.), *Literacy and young children: Research-based practices* (pp. 261–290). New York: Guilford Press.

Vygotsky, L. S. (1962). *Thought and language* (E. Hanfmann & G. Vokar, Trans.). Cambridge, MA: MIT Press. (Original work published 1934)

Wagner, R. K., Torgesen, J. K., Rashotte, C. A., Hecht, S. A., Barker, T. A., Burgess, S. R., et al. (1997). Changing relations between phonological processing abilities and word-level reading as children develop from beginning to skilled readers: A 5-year longitudinal study. *Developmental Psychology, 33*(3), 468.

Walmsley, S. (1994). *Children exploring their world: Theme teaching in elementary school.* Portsmouth, NH: Heinemann.

Wells, C. G. (1986). *The meaning makers: Children learning language and using language to learn.* Portsmouth, NH: Heinemann.

Wepner, S. B., & Ray, L. C. (2000). Sign of the times: Technology and early literacy learning. In D. S. Strickland & L. M. Morrow (Eds.), *Beginning reading and writing* (pp. 168–182). New York: Teachers College Press.

Whitehurst, G. J., & Lonigan, C. J. (2001). *Get ready to read!: Screening tool.* New York: National Center for Learning Disabilities.

Wiggins, G., & McTighe, J. (2005). *Understanding by design* (2nd ed.). Alexandria, VA: ASCD.

Wong Fillmore, L. (1979). Individual differences in second language acquisition. In C. J. Fillmore, D. Kempler, & W. Wang (Eds.), *Individual differences in language ability and language behavior* (pp. 203–228). New York: Academic Press.

Wood, D. J., McMahon, L., & Cranstoun, Y. (1980). *Working with under fives.* London: McIntyre.

Woodcock, R. W., McGrew, K. S., & Mather, N. (2001). *Woodcock–Johnson III Tests of Achievement.* Itasca, IL: Riverside.

Wooten, D. A., & Cullinan, B. E. (Eds.). (2009). *Children's literature in the reading program: An invitation to read.* Newark, DE: International Reading Association.

Yopp, R. H., & Yopp, H. K. (2000). Sharing informational text with young children. *The Reading Teacher, 53*(5), 410–423.

Index

Note: *f* following a page number indicates a figure; *t* indicates a table.